Indulgence

Dasck Eve DeFin.

New Generation Publishing

Gods or god are any of various beings conceived of as supernatural, immortal, and having special powers over the lives and affairs of people and the course of nature.

In certain other religions god is a superhuman being or spirit worshipped as having power over nature or human fortunes.

Monotheism is: the doctrine or belief that there is only one God.

God in monotheistic religions is the creator and ruler of the universe, regarded as eternal, infinite, all powerful, all knowing; Supreme Being; Almighty. God in Christianity and other monotheistic religions is the creator and the ruler of the universe and source of all moral authority.

List of Chapters

Map of the Old Languedoc.

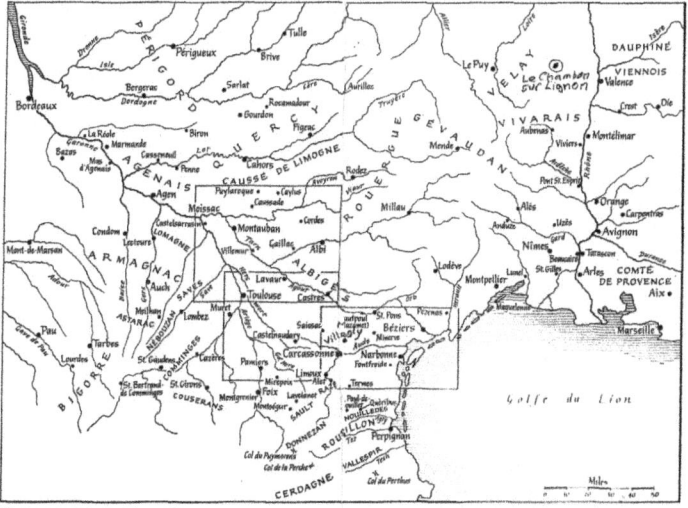

XI. Languedoc in the time of the crusade

Chapter 1.

The Cathars Crusades.

Never let the truth comes in the way of a good story.

If you have lately travelled in the Languedoc in the south-west of France you have been made aware of the Cathars. Near Carcassonne: the signs: "Vous etes ici dans le pays Cathare" or "Le chemin des Cathares" on the A9 announce that the Cathars have not finished with us yet

The Cathars were a Christian sect who settled in the region in the 9th century and disappeared in the 14th. They have been invisible and mostly unknown until a few years ago but after centuries of silence they have become popular again; books are written about them: serious researches and romances without end but none come close to answering the real question: why did they have to die?

The answer to this question brings the extraordinary discovery that the Cathars did not believe in hell. Just an opinion at the moment the study of the Cathars' destiny makes it an irrevocable reality.

For the moment this outstanding belief is hidden.

Who they were, where they came from and what they believed is part of the culture of the region; their time and place are remembered, their beliefs are familiar, incidents of their fate are recorded and the manner of their deaths is known except for their rejection of hell: a piece of information that is vital to understand them but which disappeared with the last of them.

The manner of their death is the problem. The Cathars behaved in an extraordinary way and the Vatican, and with it the Christianity of the day, supported the response of the religious world.

The first reaction of the newcomer to the knowledge of the Cathars is one of admiration. They were different and peaceful but when their behaviour at their death becomes acknowledged only total incomprehension is the possible reaction. How could they welcome their death as they seem to have done? How could they behave in this extraordinary and unacceptable way by throwing themselves in the pyres? Their willingness to die is inexplicable.

The reasons for the Christian Church to slaughter them are only explained in part and are not entirely convincing. The strange behaviour of the Cathars increases the sense of unease and mystery about them; something does not make sense.

The Cathars were hounded mercilessly and their religion was thoroughly broken-up; it disappeared completely in 1321. The huge region of the Languedoc in the South-West of France was devastated.

The clash between the Cathars and the Church of Rome was at the heart of the struggle. Prompted by the Popes a horrific crusade was mounted against the Cathars. This successful call to arms involved the whole knighthood of Europe and the aristocracy of what is now the north of France.

The Cathars' reasons to die are unknown but the reaction of the official Roman Church is also unfathomable; the crusades they instigated and the Inquisition they declared were determined and cruel if not a crime against humanity.

Many superficial, as well as serious reasons, can be found to explain the conflict but although fairly convincing they do not justify the action of the Cathars when faced with death or the determination of the Church to erase the very memory of them. When investigating the destiny of the Cathars it becomes clear that the Vatican felt it had the absolute obligation to get rid of them. The Cathars beliefs of the rejection of hell was dangerous for monotheism to the point that the Vatican was determined to do anything in its power to erase it for good.

In this long ago time faith was a necessity and the official Christian faith had the prerogative over all who lived in the Christian world; the Christian Church was powerful and in charge until the Cathars appeared and became popular.

The Cathars called themselves Christians and grew in numbers but the official Church and Catharism soon clashed; they could not survive together; there was no choice but war.

The two opponents were unevenly matched because before the start of the hostilities the Church of Rome had an added advantage which played an important role in the struggle: the ideology or beliefs of the middle age. This proved to be a major factor in the final outcome in the destiny of the Cathars.

The 12th century is an alien world now; it has specific beliefs unfamiliar and often outlandish to us. To walk into any Christian establishments of the time is to be plunged into a world of fantasy full of saints and demons which represents the actual visions and beliefs of the time.

The town of Albi at the centre of the Cathars' land gave its name to the Cathars crusades sometimes also called Albigensian wars. The cathedral of Albi, the biggest brick cathedral in Europe, started in 1278 was a powerful symbol of the prominence of the Church of Rome. Albi was chosen with care by the Holy See, located at the heart of Cathars country it proclaimed the power of the Church. The timing too is critical because the wars were at their most violent but the outcome not yet determined. The message given by the cathedral is clear: the Church will triumph. The cathedral stands for the rightness of Catholic beliefs in opposition to Cathars beliefs.

The hum of traffic, the blips of phone, the sounds of the modern city hide the past; only the pigeons flapping seem the same as in Cathars time and of course the monstrous cathedral. If you stand outside it is difficult to imagine the thoughts of a believer of the 12th century: there is too much light and space, too much knowledge and not enough fear to recapture the mood of the time. However the outside of the red cathedral gives plenty of clues; it is massive, powerful, thriving and uncompromising and announces its aim without delicacies or regrets.

It is an outrageous build, more like a fortress or a prison than the house of the Lord but it achieves its purpose and leaves no doubts about the strength and power of the Catholic Church. The overwhelming feeling it inspires is one of awe.

The Middle Ages is a strange world, the people entering the cathedral came in with a vast accumulation of beliefs and fears difficult to envisage today but we have been left evidences of what they thought, it is everywhere in and out of the cathedral, one only needs to look.

The first impact of the outside, with the massive walls high enough to reach the sky, alerts the pilgrim to the power of the Church, to its authority, its wealth and its omnipotence. If the outside is daunting the inside is welcoming. Once on the other side of the door, in the gentle shadows after too glaring a sun, the church opens its arms in the majestic space of its upside-down bell; it lets you know that, at last here, you are safe. It is luxurious with every inch of the columns and walls covered with colours: faded reds and soft blues and greys in a myriad of shapes and patterns to beguile the most wary or suspicious. The visitor is wrapped into the religious and entrapped. In this unfamiliar world the right of Christianity to the possession of the souls of men is continually reaffirmed.

The cathedral is a book without words and although the symbols around it are not immediately obvious they become visible in the confusion of details. In the inside they can be divided in two equal but opposite camps. The first reaffirms the misery of the human condition in life on earth as well as in the afterlife; life on earth is not a bed of roses and the afterlife can bring anguish but …the Church is here.

The second message explodes with the promise of happiness. The church communicates the coming of joy. The miseries in life and in the afterlife are well depicted; on earth it is recognised in the images of suffering on the paintings of the martyrdom of Saints and in the Stations of the Cross; life on earth can be dire and the various images of pain and blood are familiar for believers standing in the church.

The reality of the suffering on earth is echoed in the afterlife with the horrors of hell. In Albi the huge triptych of the Last Day of Judgment is in the nave and reminds the faithful that life after death can be horrific.

Heaven and hell are on either side of the picture of an immense God sitting on luminescent clouds for the Last Day of Judgement. The painting engulfs the end of the church. Heaven is on the right where in humans with beatific smiles in a garden full of flowers are guided by angels in white robes towards the gate of heaven; it's bliss!

While on the other side the grotesque figures and agonised faces of those who are condemned to eternal damnation are attacked by demons pushing them towards the furnace of hell. It is interesting to note that on this particular triptych the numbers of damned is greater than the numbers of saved. All this double misery is depressing but the second message of the Church erupts everywhere; the opposite joyful belief that with faith in God and the help of the priests Salvation is possible is depicted in the very essence of the building; it is majestic, powerful, and beautiful.The promise that the Church is there and will guide the believers through the turmoil of life on earth and in the afterlife is unmistakable; the guaranty of lessening the horrors of hell if not eradicating it completely is clearly indicated.

For the pilgrims of the Middle Ages the misery of life on earth was a reality; the horrors of hell were legitimate since they were paralleled to the suffering of life on earth. The afterlife with heaven and hell was seen as a representation of a comprehensible situation similar to the one on earth; the afterlife with heaven and hell made sense. The exaltation in entering a church was tremendous because the Church demonstrated that it had the power to help.

In Albi the building is huge and imposing and reminds the pilgrim of the power of the Church while the beautiful decorations, the sounds and scent of the church in the muted atmosphere, establish the feeling of safety and the promise of salvation. At last shelter from the terrors of life is possible with the aid of God and the Church. With faith and religion gathered in the Institution of the Church not all is lost, the soul can be saved and paradise reached. The Church guides and brings relief, it gives reassurances and promises. It is a shelter from the difficulties of life and a proof that heaven can be reached. Horrors as well as rewards are plastered in and around the cathedral as they were in most churches of the time. The images of horrors are purposefully traumatic, full of blood, tears, gruesome flesh and horrific pain to confirm the necessity of God. In fact the more horrific the pictures are, the more inevitable the Church is.

There were no doubts about the terrors in the afterlife. The people of the time were petrified and reminded of their frailty most days of the week. The thought of an afterlife to last for ever was only assuaged by a belief in God and the willingness of the Church to help the sinners. The Last Day of Judgement was unequivocal: God is powerful and Just: the wicked will be punished and the good people will be rewarded. The concepts entwined together work; they form a logical system difficult to deny. The nightmarish pictures were the truths of the time; the physical attacks on the body and the suffering of the souls were acknowledged with absolute conviction because they were the reality of life on earth and the accepted pictures of the afterlife. They made sense. Nobody disagreed with the premises because they reflected the known truths of the harshness of life; they were the accepted beliefs of the day and were re-enforced from birth to death. These beliefs were facts.

The riddle of the cathedral is not complicated, the clues are transparent. The paintings are terrifying and specific and talk about pain and torment to recall the conditions of humanity on earth and in the afterlife. The sufferings in the afterlife are real if...one is not saved. There is no ambiguity about what to expect; the agony is eternal and depicted with revolting, grisly, nauseating and horrendous images but more importantly the pain is inescapable.

There is no escape ...except with the Church: "Believe and you will be saved". The building is both beautiful and terrifying, the message is unambiguous: life on earth and after death is full of anguish and misery but the Church is there: the Church reassures and offers shelter and protection.

The Church does not only forewarns and reminds the believers of the sorrow of the human condition, the Church reassures and guarantees a way out; it shows the path towards redemption. The Church comforts. One must belong.

To make sure that this compounded truth was understood people's behaviour were constantly under watch; the Sunday services were not to be missed otherwise fines were issued. Confessions helped to keep in check the state of mind of the population. People were expected to behave properly, they had to be decent and worthy otherwise the punishments were horrific; and to be virtuous was not easy since humanity was believed to have a tendency towards sins. Underlining the certainty of the wrath of God was the firm belief that one was born a sinner with the Seven Deadly Sins: wrath, greed, sloth, pride, lust envy and gluttony a constant presence.

The mind set of the people, at the beginning of this first millennium, is baffling for our modern thinking because we are shielded from pain with new medicine and the sophisticated techniques of cheating death. Most people are also free from hunger in our Western countries and we live longer. In contrast life in the Middle Ages could be harsh and, for many, death came early. The world at that period for Cathars or Christians was not easy; Michael White writes in "The pope and the heretic":

"The average life expectancy was twenty-four for a woman and twenty-seven for a man. The majority of people were hungry and ill most of the time and the rich suffered most of the same horrors as the poor; plague, war and pestilence were supremely democratic. All but a few were illiterate, innumerate and spent much of their time inebriated. Most people travelled no further than ten miles from their own homes during their entire lives and were pathologically suspicious of strangers; few had an inkling of the year in which they live, nor any knowledge of the world beyond their village or town. Their religion, although Catholic, was composed of nine part superstition and earth magic to one part Mathew, Mark, Luke and John; the form of Christianity they were forced fed was barely understood, enwrapped as it was with quasi-mystical terminology. Most important the populace received its religious indoctrination in an ancient and (for most people) quite unintelligible language: Latin".

Although Michael White is talking about 1450 and much of the population of Europe had been decimated by the Black Plague the Cathars life, two hundred years before, was fairly similar. Life was hard.

Most people, terrified and ignorant, obeyed the Church. In the Middle Ages faith was a necessity and religion a light in the darkness. Fear and ignorance about the world prevailed in this unyielding climate when the Cathars first appeared. Religious beliefs ruled everything.

Two hundred years before the start of the crusades a group of thoughtful Christians listened, entranced, to monks from the east and, enlightened, changed their allegiance from the Church of Rome to this new religion called Catharism. Some Cathars' cells were formed in the north of Italy and in Germany but they settled mainly in the Languedoc this luminous region with a gentle climate. Immediately their very existence was a thorn in the flesh of the Church of Rome. The Cathars set themselves against the Vatican and were killed to the last one. But memories of them have not disappeared.

Like cautious survivors who hide in dark places till a moment of readiness the Cathar's name has reappeared now that nothing is to be feared. They have not been heard off for nearly a thousand years but they are popular again because, at last, there is no fear of reprisal. Their story fascinates because of their horrendous death but mainly because their story is unfinished because incomprehensible.

"Never men do evil so completely and cheerfully as when they do it from religious conviction"

Blaise Pascal 1623-1662.

The Albisengian Crusades.

The Cathars were pacifists and abhorred pain but they fought like tigers when they were attacked. They won a few battles but in the end they were hunted down and killed during the hundred years or so between 1209 and 1321. That year the last of their leaders was burned at the stake. At no time was a process found for understanding the other side's position between these two Christian opponents: the official Christian crowds, and in particular the priests, rejoiced in front of the pyres because, at last, the souls of the miscreants were saved for eternity and the Cathars were faithful to their beliefs and died in the pyres for reasons still unknown.

Simon de Montfort the "sword of the church" was a baron from the north of France, a military genius he was, at the beginning, the major reason for the success of the crusades in the many battles. He gained vast territories. The Pope had declared that whoever gained lands from the Cathars must keep them as their own with the moral certitude of doing right, an incentive which persuaded many to join the crusaders.

But the real extermination started before Simon de Monfort.

The now famous reply by the pope's representative: "Kill them all, the Good Lord will recognise his own" happened in the Beziers of July 1209.

I stand today looking at the quiet town surrounded by the semi-desertic garrigue in this July of 2009; it is difficult to accept that all the inhabitants were massacred: Christians and Cathars alike, 20.000 people were killed and because there was so much blood and so many bodies the chroniclers of the time talked about 100.000 dead. A successful execution.

Before the killings St Dominic is supposed to have walked up and down the streets exhorting the Catholics to change their minds and reveal the Cathars so that they could be dealt with, but to no avail. The Cathars died for their faith that day and their Christian friends and neighbours stood by them and died with them. So much blood, so much useless pain!

This was only the beginning; the rest of the Cathars history was doomed. The Cathars were attacked and fought back; many of the Cathars castles fell (often through treachery) in ferocious battles against the crusaders which ended up with the Cathars on the pyres.

The battles of the following places: the castle of Termes, Lastour, Saissac, Roquefixade, Usson, Puivert, Queribus, Peyrepertuse, Puilaufrens, Aguilar are taken, the Cathars are burned at the stake. Minerve with 150 burned– they threw themselves in the flames - and Lavaur, with 400 Cathars man, women and children burned- carries the sad record of the largest number killed in one instance.

In Montsegur 200 threw themselves in the flames also. Montsegur is an ancient ruin; a Cathar castle perched on a rocky height. Forlorn and desolated it symbolizes the fate of the people it tried to protect.

The Inquisition had intensified and many more prisoners were taken and burned. Heretics were burned; it was the law of the Church: the purifying fire washed away the sins of the heretics and the Church can say, with truth, that it did not have blood on its hands since only fire or water can be used to kill heretics.

"The Holy See never sentenced the heretics to the stake directly; with characteristic hypocrisy it always passed that duty on to a civil authority. The official statement from the Holy office to the governor of ... the interested jurisdiction was invariable:

Take him (the heretic) under your jurisdiction, subject to your decision, so as to be punished with the due chastisement; beseeching you however, as we do earnestly beseech you, to mitigate the severity of your sentence with respect to his body that there may be no danger of death or the shedding of blood. So we cardinals, Inquisitor and general, whose names are written beneath decree."

"This document from the Vatican archives was published in 1921 and with its euphemism and ambiguous language the Vatican can truthfully state that it never ordered the death of any heretics and it never shed the blood of any". Michael White. "The Pope and the heretic".

The government and Church agents who executed the order were terrified to be themselves excommunicated or burned at the stakes if they demurred; the population understood the decision since they were in the same situation.

The Inquisition.

The Inquisition existed already but was a small office before the Cathar Wars. The Crusade against the Cathars was successful but to make sure that no heretics survived in 1233 enormous power was given to the tribunals of the Inquisition. Their aim was to eliminate all heretics if they did not recant. Heresy is a serious crime:

"…heresy is to go against the official beliefs of the Christian Church".

A mild definition when the consequences are so horrendous, first excommunication: religious jargon for exclusion from the Church and from the community but more importantly, at that time, the absolute certainty of going straight to hell after death.

To assure the obedience of the people the chosen weapon of the Church was terrible.

The inquisitors were powerful and only accountable to the Pope. Popes Innocent III, Honorius III and Gregory IX gave autonomy to the Dominicans to do as they wanted. The monks in black capes were thorough.

In 1252 the Pope Gregory IX allowed the torture of suspected heretics; it simply meant that what was currently happening was now official and had the blessing of the Catholic Church.

St Dominic, a friend of Simon de Montfort, was intent in swaying the Albigensiens back to the mainstream of Christian's faith and created the order of Preachers for that purpose. Dominic may or may not have been an Inquisitor but his followers and his order of Dominicans were in charge of the tribunals and were dedicated, thorough and merciless.

With their absolute power, the repression was dreadful in the South of France. The number of Inquisitors increased; few places escaped their inspection and their word was law. Many victims were taken, found guilty, imprisoned and tortured before being put to death by flames. The Inquisitors were feared and hated. On their first visit to Moissac, a small town, the priests of the Inquisition burned 210 heretics. Many more towns and villages were investigated. Many innocent people were tortured and killed.

The Cathars were pursued and killed to the last one, their faith disappeared. The Church of Rome's violence is extreme.

The Inquisition continued for centuries to repress any hint of heresy in the population of Europe. From the small institution before the Albigiensian wars it changed into the historic movement whose influence in later centuries covered most of Europe until it was finally dismantled in the 19th century.

Not just Cathars were pursued but any who were thought to be heretics were hunted down mercilessly. Pope John XII, around 1300, authorised the Inquisition to pursue sorcery and witchcraft. Up to 70.000 thousand of witches are officially recorded but as victims were not always registered many were probably executed; some talk about millions having perished throughout Europe. They were mostly women, although there were a few men and children. Between 1500 and 1650 they were tortured and executed on the order of the Catholic Church and the Church of England. Witch-hunters were appointed by the Church of England until Oliver Crownwell (1599- 1658) put a stop to it.

The Catholic priesthood, like kings, were not allowed to draw blood so the witches were drowned or like the Cathars burned at the stake. It was only in the 17th century at the end of the witch campaigns that witches were hung. The witch hunt kept women powerless and in fear for hundreds of years.

The Albigensien Inquisition was founded with the help of St Dominic (1170-1221) and became an official Christian imposition at the end of the 12th century. The Tribunal of the Holy office of the Inquisition known as the Spanish Inquisition was established in 1487 more than two hundred years later. Of course the Inquisition did not stop between these two dates.

Dominic, the black friar, devoted the best years of his life to combat heresy; he found a copious and irreducible group in the Cathars. He worked diligently and when a heretic was deaf to argument or persuasion, he would cheerfully stand by the pyre to see him burned. St Dominic was canonised in 1234.

The Inquisition established its reign of terror for centuries and the Inquisition had the blessing of the popes: the most pious, powerful and knowledgeable leaders in religious Europe. They followed rather than led what was the accepted norm of the day; in fact they increased the incidence of tortures instead of disallowing them.

The Orthodox Church.

It could be argued that the Church of Rome was involved with such intensity and aggression against the Cathars because of its anxiety about the possible diminution in its ranks since it had suffered a terrible blow a few years previously with the definitive emergence of the Orthodox Church between 1054 and 1204. This division is more a loss of contact and a physical separation than a parting but the Catholic Church finds itself suddenly enormously diminished. No major aggression is involved with the separation of the East and West Churches but it makes the Cathars' rebellion at the same time more difficult to tolerate. The timing is unfortunate for the Cathars.

The Cathars were disbanded then exterminated, some of their writings were destroyed and their faith disappeared. It is evident that the Vatican was absolutely intent in destroying the very essence of Catharism.

Really the aggression of the Church is excessive and the behaviour of the Cathars incomprehensible. The word Cathar is a title given to them later by those who mocked them; the word comes from the Greek word

Khataros which signifies purified or pure, they called themselves "Good Christians".

The Church of Rome did not want them. It must be said that the Church tried to settle the problem peacefully before organising a crusade against them. At the beginning emissaries were sent from Rome to convince these new fanatics to change their minds and stay with the Church but the Cathars were inflexible and after more than fifty years of inconclusive meetings and failed persuasions the Church named them heretics.

The Church of Rome had numerous practical and religious reasons for its murderous campaign, reasons which have not been refuted or changed since then. It has left the memory of the Cathars to be a sad deluded group of believers belonging to a discredited Christian sect.

Chapter 2.

Salvation and Morality.

(Law and Order and the Ten Commandments.)

The reason why the Vatican had no problem enlisting allies from all over Europe against the Cathars was its unique position at the time.

The people then believed in a powerful God, a bringer of Justice who, on the Last Day of Judgement, would reward and punish with heaven and hell. The Christian world believed in a presupposed set of beliefs which led to a faith encapsulated in the concrete beliefs of the time which were universal truths. They were:

1. God exists and created the world.

2. The bible is sacred and the word of God.

3. Sin is part of the conditions of life on earth and eternal damnation is part of the afterlife.

4. The Pope is the representative of God on earth and therefore his bulls and dictum are divine commands.

5. Only the Christian Church is the link between God and humanity and only the Church can save souls.

(The last two statements apply only to the Catholic Church today).

These beliefs were not opinions based on faith but solid facts, they were not contested since they were the reality of the day; they percolated into every aspects of medieval life. The doctrine of Christianity and the decrees of the Popes reached all corners of the Christian world.

The need to avoid the wrath of a terrifying God and to preserve one's eternal soul in order to go to heaven was a constant yearning of every minute of everyday. God was real and not to be disavowed. The issue of Salvation was a major factor in the medieval period to all those who were brought up with Christian beliefs. The Church position was unassailable because of the absolute belief in the afterlife; the need to gain Salvation was a priority and possible with the help of the Church.

Salvation.

The Church, the Institution was in charge of Salvation. The Church sees its responsibility as Salvation. The Church is emphatic on its function: "Extra Ecclesiam Nulla Salus" or outside the Church there is no Salvation. This early quote from AD 253 is the essence of what the Church is about. Salvation is the gift of the Church. The strength for the Church resides in its ability to intercede with God to bring Salvation from eternal damnation. Salvation is the duty and the obligation of the Church, it is its "raison d'être" and Salvation is necessary to combat the nightmare of eternal damnation. The constant message of the Church is that Salvation is obtainable with its help.

The familiar religious buildings sit in the centre of the communities to deliver the universal Christian message; towns had cathedral and villages and small communities had their own prominent place of worship. The religious buildings were the best built and the biggest to show the power of the Institution; it emphasised its ability to intercede with God. The church was in the best position and its size and rich contents reflected the village's wealth and piety; a significant factor because it represented the chances of going to heaven. The presence of the Church (the Institution) with its priests and rituals was overwhelming; it meant that the religious beliefs, services and ceremonies were a constant presence in the life of the people. The village church was the extension of the main Institution of the Vatican and since the Popes are the representative of God on earth and the links between God and humanity the priests' words were seen as coming directly from God and were understood as orders rather than advices. The church buildings in any village were clearly visible on the outside while the inside was constantly improved with care and money for decorations; the best that the land and people could offer was added to the impact of the Church and the comfort of the priests.

To avoid eternal damnation was crucial. With the help of the Church: penances, flagellations, offerings, genuflexions and prayers were accompanied with anxiety, genuine regrets and promises to do better with the constant hope that hell would recede. The more affluent went on pilgrimages to far away places and were gone sometime for years.

A bevy of priests managed the behaviour and thinking of all humans around the religion. Religion was essential and in charge because religion controlled the outcome of the final journey after death towards heaven or hell.

The Church had an assortment of devices to make sure it was never forgotten. The tithes: a tenth of one's income was an unavoidable Church's tax and meant that the Church was immensely rich. Missing the Sunday services was followed by a heavy fine. On a more positive note extra prayers and others blessings could be asked and paid for and, from 1095 when they were first named, Indulgences, and the selling of them to those who had indulged in excesses and were destined to hell, became popular.

These little bits of paper were written by the highest religious leader of the region and promised a reduction in the punishment in the afterlife. Like points to be gained the richest and the most afraid bought as many of them as they could. Indulgences were expensive so the really poor could not afford them so had to behave exceptionally well. This suited everybody since the populace was obeying and behaving while the great of the world could do whatever they wanted and still not fear for too long a stay in purgatory if they did not end straight in heaven.

The indulgences cost money but they were invaluable in restoring the promise of heaven; in return faith and obedience to the Church were the only demands. The grip of the Church on the afterlife gave it great power on life on earth; the terror of the afterlife, with undeniable logic, reaffirmed that behaviour on earth influenced the final destination after death. The Church was the gate to heaven.

The Church was solid but in order to persuade the more reluctant who felt that the horrific punishments of hell were was a long way away in the afterlife. Excommunication was a more immediate punishment on earth and not fun. Excommunication is the expulsion from the Church a severe punishment which had immediate consequence since it excluded the transgressor from all contact in the community. Excommunication curtailed the ability to barter, to buy and to sell; any kind of activity or job became difficult if not unworkable. To continue to live in the community and have a normal life was impossible; the only escape was to leave the village and hope that another unsuspicious community, far away, would accept a stranger.

But the more terrible outcome of excommunication was the automatic certainty of hell in the afterlife. The Church was thus able to punish effectively those who did not toe the line.

The Church was in charge of men, women and children's souls and oversaw the moral conduct of everyday life; nothing happened without the approval of the priest because he could obstruct the journey to heaven and imperil one's soul. The majority who accepted the guidance of the Church were guarantied Salvation in the afterlife, the others were damned.

One's faith was totally controlled by the religious Christian's doctrine and therefore by the priests. To follow the advice of the priesthood and keep their goodwill was paramount.

Nobody objected because the undeniable logic behind the argument was obvious to all: God punished and rewarded and therefore the behaviour of each individual on earth influenced his/her final destination in the afterlife. The Church was only comforting.

Not to believe in one's own doom was not possible. The religious buildings with gargoyles like demons from hell and paintings plastered all around the churches with specific details of suffering made this difficult. The fear of eternal damnation was constantly reinforced in the weekly services as was the solution …with the Church.

Salvation in religious meaning is the saving of the soul, that is:

"its deliverance from sin and its consequences". The consequence of sin is eternal damnation.

Everybody is a sinner from birth since St Augustine (354-430) and the message is reinforced by Thomas Aquinas (1225-1274) - note the date! - the fear of the wrath of God is real; there is no exemption for the great and wealthy, no one is excluded from sinning and from its obvious consequence… except with the grace of God and the intercession of Christ through the Church.

The obedience to the priests was part of the solution which took one on the road to redemption.

Hell is real; hell is the concrete consequence of being on the wrong side of God on the Last Day of Judgement. Hell is the kingdom of the devil and a place of evil.

The devil is by definition, a slenderer or an accuser (from a Greek word); he is a supernatural entity and the personification of evil and the enemy of God and humanity. The problem of evil is great; how to reconcile the existence of evil with that of a deity who is, in either absolute or relative term, all-powerful, all knowledgeable and all compassion is impossible.

The Christians of the Middle Ages believed that the devil was real and fought with God for the possession of humanity's souls. To help God in that battle was taken for granted. Hell is the concrete representation of the abstract concept of eternal damnation. The images of hell were graphic with flesh-eating worms, flogging, unbearable thirst, isolation and darkness and visible around the Church for those who were reluctant to do as they were told. Hell was to be avoided at all cost. The priests were obeyed.

The Cathars had an easy answer in believing in a God of evil opposite to the God of goodness. Christianity accepts a lesser entity in the devil who rules hell in the afterlife and brings havoc on earth.

In those days hell was a reality difficult to avoid; God and the wrath of God were ever present but in his mercy God had given the religious Institution the means to guide the pilgrims towards redemption. Without the Church the horrors of hell were a certainty of the afterlife but with the Church Salvation was achievable: one only had to belong and obey.

The Church was certainly not saving humanity from criminals on earth or even the misery of life, the church was saving the soul so it could reach paradise or at least avoid hell for eternity by being purged in the purgatory, not a pleasant place but not eternal.

The Church and only the Church bestows Salvation; busy and willing it provides many acts of redemption: confessions, absolutions, benedictions and blessings not freely offered but available. Prayers are lead, services conducted and Indulgences sold to prove that the Church has the resources and the will to save the souls.

The Churches main concern was the saving of souls; a link between men and God it offered a road to deliverance. With the Church eternal damnation could be avoided.

The medieval world was a religious world, a busy little world but the religious authority went further because it encompassed everything, all actions, all aspects of life on earth as well.

This grip of the Church on what happened in the afterlife after death gave it great power to what happened in life on earth. The fear of hell was sufficient to insure the power of the Church whose main business was the afterlife but the Church had another asset to help it control life on earth: it had in Morality.

2. Morality.

Christianity possesses another invaluable advantage which gave it a hold on life on earth with the prerogative of morality. The Christian Church was seen as the only holder and therefore controller of morality. Only the priests, through the authority of the Popes, had divine knowledge of ethic and were able to communicate it. Thus the two concepts of Salvation and Morality gave the religious system absolute control.

The use of the powerful tool of morality was effective. The ethic of the day and with it all social and moral behaviour, from the kings to the poorest peasants, were dictated by the Church.

Morality is:

"...the principle concerning the distinction between right and wrong or good and bad behaviour".

Christianity dominated with its "ownership" of morality.

The Church has an ace which allowed it total control of moral issues, an ace that is still in place today. This amazing champion for the monotheistic religions is the list called the Ten Commandments.

The Ten Commandments.

The Ten Commandments are given directly by God; they are divine laws and they are the exclusive property of the monotheistic religions.

Although the dates are disputed Moses is supposed to have received the Ten Commandments inscribed by God on tablets of stone around 1391-1271 BCE. The tablets were initially part of Judaism but they were adopted by Christianity.

The Commandments are thus not only old and therefore to be respected but also divine and therefore inviolable.

"And the Lord said unto Moses, come up to me into the mount, and be there: and I will give thee the tables of stone, and a law and commandments which I have written; you mayest teach them." Exodus 24-12, 13.

The Ten Commandments is an extraordinary list of obvious "do and don't". What seems simple on first encounter is a sophisticated record of different elements mixed together in which the religious and the secular are cleverly combined; it is a stroke of genius.

The two irregular parts of the Ten Commandments are split between the first four instructions which have to do with the belief in a single God:

1. Believe in one God.

2. Do not make images or likeness of God.

3. Do not swear falsely by the name of God.

4. Remember the Sabbath.

They are no more than religious propaganda. And the six other rules:

5. Honour your mother and father.

6. Do not murder.

7. Do not commit adultery

8. Do not steal.

9. Do not bear false witness against your neighbours.

10. Do not covet your neighbours' wife.

are universal moral and social laws.

These last six social laws are secular laws; they are, simply, the necessary code to survive in society. They are, of course, moral laws but because of their appurtenance in the Ten Commandments they are wrongly thought to be religious laws too.

The ten admonitions in the Ten Commandments are impossible to separate because they are given as a single unit but the list mixes together religious rules with the basic laws to regulated life in society ... religious or others. These last six laws or commandments are universal, secular, essential and necessary to any social interactions but they are not religious; they only appear to be exclusively religious because they are tacked after the first four religious rules and because they are part of the religious Commandments. The marvel of the Commandments is the combination of religious and non-religious elements in a tight indissoluble list of orders.

The genius of the Commandments is to combine together the social predictable rules which govern any groups of people living together, religious or not, with the religious commands thus making all the Commandments religious including the secular moral/social laws.

Morality has been hijacked by Christianity so that morality and social behaviour are religious and rest exclusively with the Church. From then on those rules, more than three thousand years old, are divine, come directly from God, are not negotiable and are seen as unconditionally religious

The integration of these two different elements: secular in the last six Commandments but religious in the first four means that the secular necessity of the last six has disappeared swallowed by the religious intent. To augment the certainty of the right of the Church to regulate morality the "Divine Command theory" takes God's will as the foundation of ethics", a declaration taken for granted in monotheistic religions

The "Divine Command Theory" and the Ten Commandments have guaranteed the exclusivity of morality to monotheism and has been particularly used by Christianity. With this incredible asset the Christian Church was not only the custodian of morality but regulated the public laws because the civic laws, like the moral laws, were dependant on the religious will.

All together the Ten Commandments encapsulate both the monotheistic and therefore the Christian religious rules and the unavoidable moral laws of any society.

This power tool has enabled the Church to dominate the civic laws of all Christian lands for many centuries; after all what man could better God?

Thomas A Becket (1118-1170) had no hesitation; with God behind him he knew he had the most clout; he was after all the representative of God on earth and as the messenger of God he was above the king. After his assassination Henry II had to humble himself and do penance in public. The Church was above the kings because it had God on its side. The Public Laws owed its allegiance to nobody except God and God spoke through the words in the bible or the lips of the Popes.

In Christian lands Law and Order was a gift of the Church. The feudal system, with its chivalric rules: a warrior code with a moral system which asked the knights to protect children and widows, to be generous and disciplined and to fear God and maintain his Church, was intrinsically linked to the religious order.

The Church and the feudal landowners together provided order; the barons and great landlords, who were imbued with Christian beliefs, supplied arms and men and fought along side the Church who could impose the moral code; between the two they maintained the moral rules of the community. The leaders of the lands were tied to the religious system and with the Church they controlled law and order.

The Church directed the moral outlook and therefore the behaviour of the kings as well as the populace. Above the kings were the laws of God so the kings had to, like the humblest serf, obey the Commands of God. It actually meant that the highest in the land had to follow the demands of the Church. In any clash between kings and bishops the Church won every time.

The secular laws have been swallowed up by religiosity but the religious laws too have gained by their closeness to the secular laws; the religious laws have secured the hallmark of universality by their association with the necessary secular laws; a state of affair still prevalent today.

This juxtaposition and interchange have given the religious laws enormous power because they are now associated with the social/moral laws which cannot be rejected. The validity of the religious laws is greatly increased by the impossibility of dismissing the secular laws. Whoever put the Ten Commandments together created a vigorous, dynamic, stage-managed and apparently uncomplicated set of rules which still endures. The Ten Commandments, an ingenious mixture which provides both a vital publicity for monotheism and a survival kit for society, is still with us.

An outstanding achievement!

The Ten Commandments are unbeatable as an exercise in Public Relation; the manipulation of the different concepts makes it impossible to differentiate the distinct intent between the social/moral rules and therefore universal rules and the religious rules. And because they all seem to come from God they are all assumed to be religious.

The Ten Commandments is the illustration of an ultimate manoeuvring to gain a specific aspiration; they were not purposefully intended to confuse, and eventually to deceive, as they simply corresponded to the reality and the beliefs of their age.

In the Middle Ages the Church was the absolute master of social and moral behaviour because the laws of the Church, given in the Ten Commandments and in the "Divine Command theory", were religious as well as moral/social laws. These laws, in essence, guided and regulated the civil laws.

At that time to make matter worse the Ten Commandments were presented as the Church exclusive possession so that morality resided solely with the appurtenance to Christianity. The Vatican was the unique judge on ethic in all the land that Christianity had touched; Christianity controlled the laws and with it order and morality because the Church was the administrator of the Ten Commandments.

Eight hundred years ago the social rules were exclusively religious and gave the Church enormous authority and power. The Church made the laws and enforced them: a unique position with legislative and executive powers in the same hands. The Church was untouchable because the Church was the executive power too: it had the instruments to make the laws obeyed.

Rules are just jokes unless they can be enforced; the Church had a ready tool: the reward of heaven and the punishment of hell; they were powerful on an ignorant and terrified population.

To add to the medieval soup ignorance and lack of communication rendered the Church even more powerful. The way ahead without the Church is unthinkable, the Church is inevitable.

The Ten Commandments is a brilliant list which has entitled Christianity to think itself the arbiter of ethics and has allowed the Popes, even today, to have views on contraception, condoms, abortion or gay marriages without legal consultation or rational explanation. Morality is seen as exclusively Christian a conviction still taken for granted today.

A powerful legacy remains still prevails; for most people not to be Christians is to be amoral and non-Christians are often equated with immorality and lawlessness and held in fear if not contempt in very Christian countries.

To this day to disobey the Ten Commandments is to be immoral and anti-social as well as irreligious. A good Christian is a model citizen because religiosity and morality are often equated. Even today the Church of England's schools emphasize the ethical education they provide.

The impact of the Christian beliefs is still recognisable in the countries of the Western world. In many countries the Church is still partly in charge. In the UK the head of State, the Queen, is also the head of Church. The Ten Commandments are still used in everyday's life: oaths are sworn on the bible and the

Sabbath used to be sacred. The UK is a religious country in which State and Church have not been officially separated; this maintains a certain amount of confusion between the ethical authority of State and Church although the laws are not initiated by the Church anymore but the clerics of the Church of England presuppose to make political speeches on affairs of morality.

In the very religious USA it is understood that to be with God or "re-born" as a Christian can only be a political asset. In this powerful country the president of the USA has to "God bless America" at the end of important speeches; it might not have anything to do with his belief in God but in using God he affirms that he is a solid citizen who can be trusted; he tells his audience that he knows the difference between right and wrong; he reminds the crowds that he has God behind him and that with God he is a fellow with morality who can maintain law and order.

The secular part of the Commandments, the six last rules, are a necessary part of the legal system of most countries in the world because they are social/moral rules but they are still associated with religiosity in the lands were monotheistic religions have had a sway although at last the idea that morality does not mean religiosity is slowly making its way forward.

In many countries the separation between Church and State has meant that the laws can now be entirely secular. In countries without the break between religion and State the civil laws are seldom based on religious demands. The modern world does not take into account the old beliefs of an ancient time.

The laws of the land are:

"…a system of rules which a country recognises as regulating the actions of its members".

No mention of the divine in this definition; no laws are directed by the religious establishment today nevertheless some confusion remains because the old religious system is so immersed in the Western Culture. The "Canon laws" which regulate the Church organisations are not inferred here.

Confusion.

The Ten Commandments are linked to social survival in the lands where culture has been conquered by one of the three monotheistic religions and although the Ten Commandments are not mentioned and seldom used their invisible influence is still at work.

The confusion between morality and religiosity has not been completely sorted out in Christian countries. In the Christian World the Church, as an ethical supervisor, still professes to be the arbiter and exclusive holder of moral laws. The social/moral laws still appeared to have a religious necessity. Our morality is governed by the Church because it has been so for so long and because its basis is sacred in the Ten Commandments. The social/moral part of the Ten Commandments is still unreservedly confused with the religious laws since they are all so well entangled together. The Ten Commandments are seldom mentioned but they underline the ethic of the three monotheistic cultures.

To attack the Commandments is ludicrous if not insane because their secular part is a social necessity. The Ten Commandments are ancient and their holly descent guarantees their longevity and their social and moral common sense assure their survival.

The Ten Commandments have been influential but to remember that morality does not demand religions is still difficult to accept although changes have come in our modern society. Today, in many Christian countries, social laws are State laws and do not demand the agreement of God to be passed but for most religious believers morality is exclusively religious.

The misconception that moral laws have to be religious still lingers in many monotheistic religious groups where it is taken for granted that the religious rules are the only ethical rules.

Today not to understand the clever integration of the two different sets of laws in the Ten Commandments and know that the Commandments carry an element of deceit in their structure rather than their content is to remain mystified. It is to be confused between religious laws and civil laws. It is the unfortunate situation in some Islamic countries where the moral laws are seen as exclusively religious.

The combination of social/moral laws enmeshed in the divine gives absolute power to the religious factions. This was the reality of the Christian Middle Ages and is still the norm in some Muslim countries where a small number of people have absolute authority on the system of laws which must be obeyed in the name of God. The Ten Commandments are, by design or fluke, an ideal platform for omnipotence.

The Muslim believers are still interpreting the will of Allah as it suits them and are therefore trapped in a system of laws that have to be religious. Islam has not untangled its religious laws from its social/moral laws yet which can result in catastrophic judgements. For Islamic believers this confusion means that the religious laws are still used as the civic laws of the land.

Sharia's laws are religious laws dealing with the topics of crimes, policies and economics which are interpreted by Islamic judges with the help of the Koran. The judges- only men- do not show extreme indulgence in their moral and civic decisions since their guide and Supreme Being: Allah is like the God of the Christian, fair but harsh in his punishment in the afterlife with hell. The punishments on earth must reflect this intent. In the end the rule of the Imam is obeyed because it is convenient; it gives power to those who can control the laws. The men of Allah interpret the laws of their God; the women try to survive the consequences. The decision to appoint only men to high offices and situations of importance take half of the available intelligence and skills out of the equation.

Suicide bombers are prepared to die in order to avoid hell. The fear of hell, never mentioned, is translated by a desire for heaven. Paradise, approval by the community and martyrdom in their own lands make suicide bombers children of Allah doing Allah's will; it is an extraordinary outcome since they break the Commandment: "you shall not kill" but their action is a sort of proselytising as it shows the strength and in their mind, the truth of their beliefs worth emphasising for the greatness of Allah.

Religion can wrap the believer in a web of illogical thinking and actions.

The interpretation of the will of God or Allah depends on the time, the place and the culture in which it happens. God is flexible.

Chapter 3.

Christianity and Catharism.

The Christianity of the medieval period did use the word Catholic but the word of Greek origin, which means universal or all embracing, came into the vocabulary in the 2nd century, Christians were Catholics in the west and Orthodox in the west. Catholics are members of the Catholic Church. The Catholic priesthood are members of the Catholic hierarchy. The Vatican is the siege of the Pope and papal authority. The Holy See is the papacy or the papal court. The Church of Rome is: "a particular organisation, typically one with its own clergy, buildings and distinctive doctrine". Institution is: "…a society or organisation founded for a religious….purpose."

Christians are believers in Christ's divinity.

The Cathars put themselves outside the official Christian Church by rejecting the divinity of Christ. It is fair to say that by that simple statement they were outside Christianity although they insisted on calling themselves Christian. Not only did they reject the Christian Church but in doing so they rejected the whole of medieval society. Their belief soon became clear, and they would not desist! They were doomed.

There is nothing new about genocide but several elements make the Cathar's one different if not bizarre. Obviously the extermination of the Cathars has been kept well hidden by the religious powers but more importantly, at all time, even now, the Church avoided all criticisms about the viciousness of its campaign and escaped all disapproval from devoted Christians. It is understandable that the Holy See would be extremely annoyed by a sect pretending to be Christian while flaunting the most important dictate of the religion but from there to exterminate them all is a step too far.

It was easy to gain the help of the barons and the populations of the Western Christian World because the danger posed by the Cathars impacted not only on the doctrine of Christianity and also on the whole of society. The Church had the authority and power to keep the campaigns going until success was met.

The really extraordinary factor in the puzzle is the behaviour of the Cathars because when they were caught they accepted their horrendous death rather than change their faith. The Cathars were gentle people so the real reason for their annihilation is not entirely resolved; the question why they could not exist along side the official Christian Church is not clear. Although many explanations can be found for the Crusades against them as well as the action of the Holy See none are totally convincing.

The beliefs and the popularity of the Cathars worked against them but the culture of the time, the environment and the dominance of the Church were factors which allowed the extermination of this religious group without opposition.

A great part of Christian Europe approved and joined in with the exhortations of the Vatican because the religious world – an exclusively Christian world at that time and place – accepted the prevalent reasons of the unsuitability of the Cathars. One of the more visible factors against the Cathars was their lack of obedience to the Christian Church while proclaiming themselves, erroneously, as Christian. Heresy against them was soon declared.

Once called heretics the Cathars were easy victims and the Church gained a modicum of legitimacy for their extermination. Excommunication was immediate. To be burned alive should have turned back the newly converted Cathars but even with this horrific punishment few of them recanted. This is an extraordinary outcome. The killing was total and vicious.

What is quite unexpected is the viciousness of the punishment. The Church today praises itself for its compassion but when its power was challenged it had no hesitation: it was brutal and merciless.

At the time of the Cathars those with more compassion were persuaded for the need of the extermination because morality and social order were essential and the sole prerogative of the Church. Social stability was imperative and it rested exclusively with the Church; to abandon the Church was to abandon law and order, to abandon the Church was to abandon an ethical way of life. Without the Church there was no social order and no moral order.

The State laws or public laws were religious laws and were backed by the rich landowners who followed their feudal rules with the medieval chivalric code.

The aristocracy imbued with religious ethic helped in the maintenance of the religious rules and thus a vicious circle was created which left the Church in the middle of the power system and in complete control.

Other factors, which make the reluctance of the Cathars to return to the official Church surprising, are the numerous gifts that the Church offered; once you belonged to the religious club there were advantages: the relief from anguish about eternal damnation was palpable in the house of God and the churches were beautiful and welcoming. It is true the horrors of hell, with flames, devils and incredible pain were depicted by the priests from their podium in graphic images but these were accepted realities; hell was part of the everyday life of the Christians; it imposed a need for Sunday services, prayers and hair shirts but the Church was there to grant its blessings.

To entice the people into the churches the buildings were made to look, sound and smell good. It was not difficult for the Church to inspire this fascination; the populace entered the religious buildings with amazement. Immediately the impact was unfamiliar with the scent of strong, exotic spices which assaulted the senses, the divine music, the stunning windows, the numerous decorations and sculptures in rich colours and the outlandish garments of the priests added to the feelings of complete and strange out-of-the body experiences.

These beautiful luxuries were promised as a reward for those who followed the Church's advice; all would be well for those who obeyed. The treasures in the church did not only reflect the glory of God they were a glimpse of the paradise to come. The church was a window on what could be expected in heaven. The convincing gift of Salvation was pure relief and the magic of the religious pageantry was overwhelming on a poor and uneducated populace. The wonder eased obedience easier. To gain for oneself what the church revealed and gave was taken for granted.

This vision of an unknown but unattainable world, recreated in the church buildings and posing as a reflection of the attainable when in heaven, was the more tempting since monsters were never far away out there. The people lived in a frightening world; their ignorant knowledge filled the distant woods with repulsive monsters capable of atrocious cruelty. For most people life was a mystery when they thought of the outside of their restricted surroundings. Life out there was baffling because unknown; even the more educated added strange creatures at the edge of the world when they drew the first map known in the Western world: the Mappa Mundi in 1300 which represented the sum total of the knowledge of the known world.

The physical and geographical world outside the village was a mystery full of horrors; it was reflected in the miseries of the afterlife in hell. The imagination, already excited by stories brought by travellers from other part of the country, was increased ten fold when hell was pictured.

The afterlife, like life on earth, was full of obstacles and challenges; if good things as well as bad were happening on a daily basis on earth them good things as well as bad were presumed to be the reality of the afterlife. Hell, with all its horrors, was not doubted. Hell and heaven were together and represented an inescapable reality.

The afterlife was a guarantee from God and an unavoidable truth; the afterlife with heaven and hell was a reflection of life on earth with the good and the bad. People, scared and ignorant, obeyed the Church... except for the Cathars.

The Church took care of the social order so it is not surprising that many devoted Christians were worried with the appearance of the Cathars. Law and Order and an ordered society might dissolve into anarchy without the hold of the Church. The principles of Law and Order touched the population at large and many were frightened that, without the Church, chaos would prevail.

The Church engendered some restraints in social behaviours; the continuation of social order was only possible with the Church; without the Church social order would disappear. The Church ruled on earth as well as in the afterlife.

The Cathars on the contrary seemed to have had little to counteract the official religion; their beliefs were different but not outstanding but surprisingly they became more and more popular.

To be a Catholic in the Languedoc of the 12th century was to have made the decision to stay with Christianity rather than to follow Catharism. On the surface the inducements offered by the Church were overwhelming while the reasons to become a Cathar were unclear and still are.

It is easy to understand why staying with the official Church was a positive option; the Church gave many benefits; Christianity itself had a lot to recommend it; it must be remembered that in those days not only was the afterlife scary since devils from the dark place of hell were sent to trap the unwary and pull them towards hell but also life on earth was complicated and bewildering because most people believed that the unknown lands just over the horizon were dangerous: hideous monsters populated these mysterious places and the fear of them was real.

It was possible for the Church to comfort the populace; the constant messages of eternal fires were not easily forgotten but the Church reassured its faithful followers not only on the outcome in the afterlife but also in the life of everyday on earth. Everybody needed the Church and everybody used the Church to pray, attend services, genuflex and cross themselves. The Church was the life-centre of the community where, on a regular basis, markets of all kinds took place everyday and where the opportunity to meet friends and have social interactions with others was added to the possibility of getting and giving news; dealing with the world outside one's home happened at the church where gossip and dealing occurred under the vigilant eyes of the priests.

The Cathars

It is in this solemn and prevailing climate that the Cathars appeared and set themselves against a mighty opponent; they did so without hesitation although they knew that the Church was powerful. By simply not obeying the Church Laws the Cathars immediately appeared dangerous since their ideas could lead to social anarchy. It was easy to accuse them and to harass them because they were seen as attacking the fabric of society. There was no alternative but to belong to the Church; to think that the Cathars could endanger the well organised system provided by the Church brought panic to all.

There were many reasons why the Church took the upper hand in provoking the Crusades against the Cathars but the most crucial reason has been eradicated from the Cathars manuscripts and is not exposed.The Cathars were extremely dangerous by their very presence; they undermined the Church and Law and Order.

A series of visible, central problems faced the Church. These recognisable reasons were both major and minor. The two major problems:

1. The rejection of the Christian incarnation.

2. Dualism.

They were important because they opposed what was fundamentally Christian. The other difficulties were relatively minor:

3. Mockery of the Cathars.

4. The growing numbers of new adherents.

5.and the clarity of the Cathars' doctrine.

The first two problems directly attacked the dogma of Christianity.

1. Christian Incarnation.

Incarnation in Christianity is the most crucial belief of the religion; it is what makes it Christianity. Incarnation is the belief that Jesus Christ son of God "became flesh" by being conceived in the womb of a woman. Jesus, thus, is both man and God.

"And the word became flesh, and dwelt among us.

John 1:14.

67

The Cathars venerated Christ and called themselves Christian but they could not recognised Christ as the son of God because he was not entirely spiritual. Christ was tainted by flesh and therefore too close to the material world by being born of a woman. Christ, in part, belonged to matter and matter was evil for the Cathars. But as Christ is closer to the world of the spiritual than mere humans he is honoured. The Cathars venerated Christ and recognised his message of love.

By not acknowledging Christ as the Messiah and the son of God the Cathars were challenging a belief central to Christian theology. The problem was insurmountable for the Vatican.

2. Dualism.

One of the most important beliefs of the Cathars was their dualism, by believing in two distinct gods they disturbed the sacred belief in the single god of the official Christian Church and set the seal to their destruction. Dualism was at the same time the strength and the curse of Catharism. Dualism is an anathema for the monotheist religion of Christianity. The enormous sin of the Cathars in dividing the vision of the divine is unforgivable. Dualism demeans the Glory of God; it splits the power of the one true God in two; it diminishes it and belittles it.

A single god encompassing all power and glory in one entity gives this unique God immense authority and legitimacy; the Church worships this unique God and gains power and credence from its exclusive position, the greater the God the more powerful the priests, the greater the God the greater the Church.

Monotheism is the basis of Christianity and the Cathars thought it was a good joke.

To make the abomination even worse the Cathars called themselves; "Good Christians" while believing in two gods. Such abhorrence was the ultimate sin and sin is by definition a crime against God; dualism made the Cathars absolute sinners.

In believing in more than one god the Cathars broke the most important decree of a single God which defines Christianity. The dualism of the Cathars appeared like an intellectual regression, an insult to the true God of the Christians and of monotheism. Dualism made the accusation of heresy a reasonable justification for excessive retaliation; the idea of a single God was well established and not negotiable.

The concept of a unique god was not new; it emerged first with the sun-god of Akhenaton around 1300 BCE. The belief did not survive the death of the pharaoh. Round 600 BC the belief in one God reappeared in the Middle East and was the revolutionary belief of Judaism; it became the foundation of what are today the three monotheistic religions: Judaism, Christianity and Islam.

This single God concept is of such importance that the first four Commandments in the Ten Commandments, the basis of monotheistic beliefs and laws, deal exclusively with this point, the rule is repeated 4 times: 1. Believe in one God. 2. Do not make images or likenesses of God. 3. Do not swear falsely by the word of God. 4. Remember the Sabbath.

It is one of the most vital elements of monotheistic religions.

Incarnation and dualism were such immense obstacles to the religious doctrine of Christianity that to accuse the Cathars of heresy was easy.

3. Mockery.

If the Cathars had been quiet and had kept their beliefs to themselves, instead of spreading them around and becoming increasingly trendy, the outcome might have been different but the Cathars were infuriating. By refusing to belong to the official Church they were seen as lacking respect even as mocking the solemn Institution.

This is a continuous irritation on a daily basis when, not only do the Cathars refuse to pay their tithes, a lot of money to give to the Church, but they laugh when threatened with excommunication. They flaunt the Holiness of the Church publicly with their insolence and no punishment touched them. They were becoming too noticeable, their mockery was exasperating and no punishment or fear of eternal damnation or excommunication made them change; nothing frightened them and their behaviour was making the true Church look ridiculous.

4. Numbers.

Their number grew as more and more loyal Christians became Cathars. Large numbers of Christians changed their faith before the crusades and the Inquisition started; they became Cathars so that the greatest part of the Languedoc was under Catharism. The Comte de Toulouse (1148-1249) was the feudal lord of the Languedoc and in sympathy with the Cathars; other landowners joined him and in doing so immediately overset the unwritten rule that only the Church of Rome had a prerogative on the population. A quiet revolution had started which competed with the Church of Rome.

5. Simple theology.

Less in the forefront but of value for the more dedicated to the meaning of the doctrine is the clarity of the Cathars' dogma; it appeals to the more sophisticated and attracted many. The simple, clear faith of the Cathars was intellectually satisfying and devoid of paradoxes and contradictions while Christianity was complicated.

In the Cathars' doctrine everything fitted: God was good and saved.

In Christianity God is powerful and judges to give punishment or reward. For the Cathars evil existed but was contained on earth.

In Christianity evil is on earth with injustices and misery and in the afterlife with hell. For the Cathars injustice and therefore criminals were taken care of with re-incarnation: a non-violent punishment.

In Christianity God punishes on earth with torture and in the afterlife with torture. The Cathars were asked to behave in a sober, pious and peaceful ways, their Bonshommes were guides who did not get rich; there were no ceremonies, no hierarchy in the priesthood and women had the same status as men.

In Christianity the priests are incomprehensible masters who mystify and punish those who do not obey.

All together there were enough valid reasons to justify the Vatican in the eye of Christian Europe and enough justification for Christian Europe to join forces with the Church. Together they formed an invincible force which assaulted the Cathars till none were left and their faith died. Of course for many Christians their religion is stimulating and intriguing; Christianity is full of ambiguities and paradoxes; the challenging questions create tension and give the religion an extraordinary dynamism. Christianity obliges one to think.

When gathered together the amount of reasons for the disruption of the Cathars is impressive; they gave plenty of convincing evidences to Christendom for the rightness of the Church's actions although some of those minor reasons might have been eventually tackled by the Institution … maybe…But the two major differences of Christian Incarnation and dualism were unsolvable.

The Cathars were their own worst enemy in being too visible by proclaiming to be the true children of God and claiming noisily to be Good Christians. They left the Christian Institution which protected humanity from the worse abuse of criminality and set themselves against a strong opponent who, they knew, was master everywhere and approved of by all. It does not make sense.

The Cathars were setting themselves in direct opposition to the Church of Rome at a time when the Church was invincible. What possible reason could have tempted these gentle people to put their head in the noose when the only outcome was death?

To flaunt official Christianity was to push the Vatican beyond what was acceptable. Heresy will have the triple advantage of condemning the Cathars, re-establishing the grandeur of the single God and preventing condemnation of the Vatican.

To make matter worse the Cathars were ambiguous about Christ resurrection. The Church had enough justifications to carry on without being impeded and the Vatican was not tolerant.

The Church, with the approbation of most believers, decided to exercise all its might to get rid of the Cathars and their beliefs. The Church certainly acted with resolves, even audacity, to get rid of them; it was also cruel and implacable. The Cathar Wars were effectively a faith-cleansing exercise which was totally successful.

The Church of Rome was thorough; men, women and children were killed, the writings destroyed and the special beliefs of the Cathars forgotten. The reasons for the extermination of the Cathars gave the Church powerful justifications to accuse them of heresy; these explanations were convincing enough to persuade the Christians of the time to let the Church do what it recommended; it was particularly so for those outside the Languedoc who did not know anything about the Cathars input.

The list of justifications was long enough for the Church to gain the help of religious Europe without having to divulge the real reason for the extermination. The Vatican must have believed that the numerous reasons were literally "God sent" since it saved the Holy See from divulging the real secret. It was after all God's will. God was on the side of the true Church, a final validation which allowed the Popes to sleep in peace and indulged themselves with a clear conscience. This meant that over the centuries there were enough convincing justifications to prevent anybody from looking further. The Church was left to slumber without demands of explanation after the mission was accomplished. The Church reigned. But not for the Cathars.

The secret of the Cathars is still hidden from most people and to say that they did not believe in hell is meaningless until the consequences are made clear. The Cathars belief would have destroyed Christianity in the 12th century. It is as valid today and therefore as dangerous as it was then.

Christianity is influential and popular and is one of the most prevalent religions on the planet today thanks to the concealment of the Cathars' real danger. It has permitted the Church to retain its power and authority intact. Well established, secure and confident the Church is with us with full authority.

Chapter 4.

The Goodies of Christianity.

Not all Christians became Cathars even before the start of the Crusades.

The appeal of the Cathars was strong but it was not enough to persuade everybody to change their faith. Many Christians stayed Christian because Christianity is attractive. Christianity is full of rewarding features, it has a long list of "Goodies" which gives a wholesome feeling of reassurance and happiness. Christianity has a lot to offer. And the Goodies are impressive. Christianity is a popular religion which has reached most corners of the world for good reasons.

In a crowd of believers the voices are robust and joyous. The words and sentences, feelings and ideas express happiness. Listen: security, support, feeling safe, contentment, safety, comfort, satisfaction, a father who takes care, availability of immense love: a love that can be given without fear of loss, love returned, feelings of adoration, bliss for ever after, the necessity of God, answers to questions, the certainty of human purpose on earth, and the conviction that morality is under control- thanks to God- all these are part of the happiness that Christianity gives. If you have met serious believers you have been made aware of most of these feelings and beliefs.

The certainty and happiness are re-enforced by the knowledge that there are no strings attached except to simply believe. Christians and Muslims like most true believers are special because they feel protected; God or Allah guard over them and this conviction does not have to be proven endlessly. Whatever happens, be it good or bad, helpful or tragic the final outcome of any situations is the correct one because, in the end, God knows better. It is the will of God. This certainty relieves difficult moments and foresees the future with a more constructive approach. The feel-good factor is constantly confirmed by the social encounters of the necessary Sundays' get-together. Meeting friends in "built for the purpose" buildings, where new comers are welcomed and where the circle of friends can be extended in the absolute knowledge that all have the same attitude, is a safe and pleasant way to spend the time. The satisfaction of ceremonies in trusted congregations, the knowledge that one belongs to a special club; the virtuous impulse to follow one's better nature without impediments or being laugh at produce gratification. What better to help somebody in need to make one feel good! The certainty that somebody is there in time of crisis, that if a call for help is made, an immediate response can be expected, creates warm feelings and gives confidence to those who now know they are not alone.

The goodies of Christianity make a long and rewarding list. Christianity satisfies the dreams, answers human cravings and in ceremonies, traditions, arts and culture provides a venue and frame for essentials events. And to top it all it has the added advantage of morality. Morality is an important bonus which persuades the believers that they are right to be Christian.

If you could make a wish list, like children make at Christmas, a spiritual list which contained what humanity desires, the following demands would look like this:

1. To live for ever,

2. To be loved by a trustworthy person or entity and to love in return.

3. To have ultimate Justice.

4. To have an answer to the purpose of life on earth and answers to questions about the creation.

Some believers might object to the order and the briefness of the catalogue since not all wishes are included, particularly the physical ones like health, but in an exclusively spiritual list many central wishes for life on earth cannot be included.

Nevertheless the four statements above are desirable and cover a wide range of spiritual necessities; they are the common denominators of monotheistic religions.

And Christianity gives it all.

1. The afterlife.

The most emotional item on the list and the most enticing is the first one: to live for ever! A dream come true! The physical evidence on earth denies the possibility of rebirth but to have an eternal soul is an acceptable solution. The words are clear:

"I tell you the truth, those who listen to my message and believe in God who sent me have eternal life."

John 5.24.

"Eternal" and "life" are words vague enough to leave doors open to the imagination, tempting enough to be believed. The resurrection, a concrete story, makes the concept of eternal soul real and recognizable. Christ, the son of God is resurrected. Christ is a man who lives after his death therefore the resurrection is genuine and authentic and life after death is a promise that can be trusted. To defeat death is the ultimate desire; Who can cope with death? Never to see the loved ones again is unbearable. Anything that can help that loss and pain is worth it.

One's own death is not fun either: it is the definitive end no one wants. The firm promise that death is not final is reassuring, even cheering. The comfort brought by the prospect of meeting loved ones again, with the possibility of having guilt assuaged and regrets readjusted, can induce feelings of joy and exaltation. To think that all will be put right and reconciliations become possible is comforting, even elating. Expectancy, the waiting time before a happy event, is often the most intensely pleasurable. Happiness knows no bond; anticipation can gallop and acquire rosy tints; imagination brings a flow of constant if subdued well-being. The expectation of heaven is present everyday of one's life… if you believe.

Nobody looks forward to their death but knowing that paradise is at the end of life makes the vicissitudes of daily toil more bearable. A life on earth looking without fear toward the ultimate delight of heaven encloses everyday in a cloud of optimism; a state good for the mind and good for the health.

Some medical staff even concedes that believers in hospital do better medically than other patients. Even with studies to back up this statement it must be taken with some scepticism; the reporters may not be intentionally prejudiced but unconsciously influenced by religious beliefs and the acquired culture. More substantial proofs are needed... if they are possible to be obtained. Nevertheless it has to be accepted that the absolute belief in the afterlife causes positive emotions in its believers. This upshot is the result of knowing that death is not final, a conviction enhanced today since only heaven is considered.

In truth death is so final that anything that can alleviate it seems worthwhile. This is Christianity great strength; it is reasonable that believers are loath to abandon the idea of living forever even if the virtualisation of paradise is hazy.

For non believers the principle of continuation is what matters a principle that is called life.

With the resurrection death is proven not to be final; the end of one's own precious being is postponed, even cancelled. After death paradise awaits: a place of delight and peace with God Almighty. Who cannot be tempted? Who cannot be persuaded?

God is here for all and in His goodness He will provide what He has the power to give: eternal life.

2. To have love. A father.

To believe in God and be a Christian makes one feel happy not only because the end of life is deferred but also because one feels safe: a father-figure watches over one; "Our father, which are in heaven…"

Not to be alone… ever is comforting; religion is a security blanket; God the father cares and looks after his creation.

"How great is the love the Father has lavished on us that we should be called children of God!

1 John 3:1.

God listens and gives:

"Ask, and it will be given to you, seek and you will find; knock and it will be opened to you." Matthew 7.7.

Unlimited love is the reward to those who believe. A love is received and given in a constant converter-belt of prayers and intercessions which can flow to the ether unimpeded. God listens and answers. God is easy to love. God is always there and available and God does not bite back... if one believes. God does not always answer appropriately but the guarantee of his love assures that however gruesome an act has been committed no retaliation will ensue, God will continue to love, especially if one confesses before one's death with a priest and Holy Rights and expresses genuine regrets, the forgiveness of God is assured.

In comparison to love a person or an animal on earth is to take an immense risk to loose them through defection or death. When this happens hearts are broken, an agonizing void is left; the pain is horrendous and long lasting. Love on earth gives wonderful rewards but it also brings the most intolerable pains when it goes wrong. There is no gamble with the love of God because his presence is absolute and total. To pray or talk to God at anytime for any length of time is rewarding. To love God is to be safe from pain or reprisal. God is not vengeful; on the contrary God is love in modern Christianity so there is nothing to fear in giving one's love to God.

3. Justice.

Justice is given, the ultimate Justice of God, inescapable and unconditionally fair.

God sits in the Last Day of Judgement and gives Justice:

"And I saw the dead, great and small, stand before God; and the books were opened and another book was open, which is the book of life, and the dead were judged out of these things which were written in the books according to what they had done."

Revelation 20:11-12.

God judges each individual fairly with the proof of personal deeds in the book of life. Nothing escapes God and Justice depends only on one own actions.

"All the nations will be gathered before him and he will separate people one from another…"

Gospel of Matthew.

"Then He will also say to those on the left hand: Depart from Me, you cursed, into the everlasting fire…."

Matthew 25-40.

God brings Justice to all believers. Those who know nothing about Him, those who are not baptised, even new born babes, will incur his wrath and end up in hell. This is not a pleasing example of the love of God but the only thing asked is not difficult, one only had to believe. One must believe to reach paradise.

4. The creation.

God also offers a solution for the creation of the universe. The Creation of the universe, with the great mysteries of where we come from and why we are here, are answered by God.

"In the beginning God created the heavens and earth."   Genesis 1.1

"The God who made the world and everything in it is the Lord of heaven and earth…"

Act 17.24.

God gives answers which makes sense of the world. To know what it is all about, why we are here, how it

87

started are impossible questions. Not to know is exasperating, to find any answer is satisfying; to find an answer which makes some kind of sense is all that is required. And God made man:

"So God created man in his own image…"

Genesis. 1.2.7.

And God gave man a purpose:

"As for you, God blessed them and said to them: Be fruitful and increase in number, multiply on the earth …"

Genesis. 1.28.

Man, from now on, with the help of God knows why he is on earth for; he has a reason for his existence and a goal. And he/she has a father to guide and to help in the venture and God is always there. To be Christian is to be solid, to have a purpose, and to be loved.

A love that is given received and returned.

The Goodies of Christianity make Christians happy. A deep seated happiness is a consequence of being Christian. Many things are missing from the list and each of us could find a pressing desire to add to it but the list must be spiritual not physical and therefore enough to eat, a major problem for so many, cannot be included. God's rewards are to do with the spiritual.

The Institution.

This is not all. Christianity is not just a dogma. Over the years the Institution has developed around the doctrine of Christianity to become a solid monument which caters for the more materialistic wishes of society: realistic support in time of grief; health, education and assistance as well as a circle of friends and the possibility of doing good work without being mocked.

The Institution is also concerned with the routines of life: ceremonies take care of the rituals: baptism, marriages, funerals even confessions solidify the need for God and give it reality. Confessions are psychological help which allay guilt or repair damaged psyche. Their imposed need was useful in keeping control of the population as well but they played a positive role in allowing people to talk about personal problems to a stranger; it helped to allay guilt. Worries that are shared alleviate the burden and the secret disclosed are never revealed. The priests keep the conversations in the confessional to themselves and therefore nothing is known by the rest of the community. Confessions still exist but they are not the negative intrusion they used to be... at least I hope so.

To put the icing on the cake Christianity, like the other monotheistic religions: Judaism and Islam, demands generosity from its believers who comply with numerous "good works".

"Good Works", performed by millions of believers all over the world, confirms that, in our modern area, God is love. "Good works" provide an access for the gentle minded - most people of the world- to follow their generous impulses and help those in need.

The first schools, the first hospitals, the first charitable gestures were started by religious movements around religious establisments. Many charitable works still are.

Thousand of compassionate acts are performed everyday by the parish priests or ministers who wait with patience and devotion for those he/she can help... because of the love of God. The priesthood is not alone; individuals or religious communities care for those who need the small acts which make a difference. There is no doubt that the Synagogues, the Churches and the Mosques gather good people who are prepared to help those less fortunate than them in the name of God or Allah.

The churches throughout the Christian lands are outlets for care and dedication to those who are frail or bereft or in need of help. Religious services are daily available to succour those who ask.

Christianity gives all the "Goodies" and has wrapped it up in the ceremonials, rituals and traditions that cater for daily needs. It is difficult not to want this religion. How can one not be happy with what it promises and answers?

It is much easier to be a Christian today as God is love. The God of the 12th century gave Love and magic but was terrifying as well; obedience was not contested.

The array of beliefs or other religions and philosophies were limited but it was irrelevant as choices were not available and most people were grateful to the Church.

The dire life of the population was lit by the hours in the church. It was the only place where display of luxuries and pageantry was accessible to the people. Sunday services were lavish and extraordinary entertainments in the drab life of the time. Money was spent in churches for the love and respect due to God.

The churches could be dazzling and the spectacles surrounding the rituals were extraordinary.

The stories and the music, the incomprehensible Latin words delivered with solemnity in inspiring buildings where coloured windows and sumptuous decorations, heavenly music, candles, incense, chanting words and priests in robes produce a mesmerizing show. The slow pace and the respected figures demonstrated the seriousness of the spectacle. To be surrounded by a crowd of people all intent on the same prayers was overwhelming.

Not only the services affected the senses but emotionally and intellectually they had the seal of approval from the illustrious and distinguished leaders of the land. Not to believe took a stubborn or dangerous mind, not to be overawed took a sceptical mind. The beliefs, the words, the stories add to the pageantry.

"… The artistic breath was what made us believe. The artistic breath gave the stories their glory and their power." Jennifer Johnston in "Grace and Truth".

With its amazing spectacle which fed the senses and the mind, the Church services were difficult to forget; to desire anew the lavish spectacle of a Catholic service in an important cathedral on a special day was taken for granted. Every body went to the big or little churches; it was the highlight of the week.

The mystifying words: Ascension, Assumption, Redemption, Trinity, Resurrection or Holy Spirit are not easy concepts; used with gravity and in amazing and inspiring buildings they were nothing but the truth even if, often, little comprehension accompanied the ceremonies and the words; one still felt up-lifted.

The difficulty of words and ideas added to the impact of the services. Peace and reassurance were the results of the strangeness and beauty of the Sunday mornings. Going to church was an enthralling experience, a welcome change from daily life from the dire world around. Life was tough and the services transported one in a world of splendour, magic and mystery and gave hope against the monsters outside.

Today the services have less impact than in the 12th century and some Reformed Churches, in order to eliminate the sensuous effects of the services, are plain if not dull. The decorations and sensuous additions to the services were perceived as the temptation of the devil and were therefore discarded. These congregations in plain even boring buildings pride themselves on their more intellectual approach which, they think, takes then closer to God.

In the context of the 12th century a Christian Church looked good, smelled good and sounded good. The stories of glory sculpted and painted on its walls added to the mystery and the excitement.

The Old Testament is a compilation of stories which depict human behaviours; they are not the best models for decency, as Richard Dawkins says:

"Those of us schooled from infancy in his ways (the God of the Old Testament) can become desensitised to their horrors".

Horrors they may be but they are recognisable stories and their universality and revolting attractions have made them an enduring success. The Old Testament is fascinating and encompasses so many different situations that it is possible to find an answer to any queries; at least some zealots are persuaded of that.

The stories in the Old Testament are realistic and terrifying at times; they give a frisson of fear which is enjoyable because there is no danger, they are only stories of a long time ago which explore the aspects of humans activities.

Christianity is stimulating and intriguing; full of ambiguities and paradoxes and with challenging questions in its dogma; it creates tension and gives the religion an extraordinary dynamism. Christianity obliges one to think.

Theologians will continue to try and unravel the numerous incongruities of Christianity and add to the long list of queries and puzzles to be explored in books and sermons.

Not only these feel-good factors have contributed to the success of Christianity but the mantel of respectability given by the Church – who dares being ostracized from their community with excommunication? -has added to its longetivity to such an extent that the idea of thinking outside the Church is still inexistent for the many who have been brought up, from a young age, with the strong catechism of the religion.

A Christian in the 12th century had to abide by the laws of the Church; to jump out of this glass bowl was not an option. God and the Church's instructions were as solid as the stones of the massive church buildings, as real as the sculptures and paintings on the walls and as exciting as the scented air and music. The Church was invincible.

The status of Christianity throughout the ages has hardly changed even with the Inquisition, the crusades, its continuous exterminations of Jews and the religious wars behind it. What is remembered is its offering of happiness and support and the fact that it is available everywhere and that it brings love ... if you belong!

When a certain numbers of assumptions have been accepted Christianity presents a coherent dogma. Immersed in Christianity the believer is in a bubble that he cannot walk out off without the great loss of many advantages and protection.

To make it more compelling Christianity is now sending an unlimited message of love and morality to all believers. The viciousness of the crusades against the Cathars and the terrible Inquisition, the rejection of Jews, the 16th century aggressive and brutal religious wars, the moral blackmail against those who did not behave accordingly, all these discretions from compassion which revealed the darker side of the strict beliefs, are long past and never referred to. Christianity's new message is one of love.

Chapter 5.
The Cathars' faith.

Catharism flourished for two hundred years before the Cathars were annihilated. From the beginning the behaviour of the Cathars and the dogma of their religion were in direct conflict with Christianity. They noisily communicated that they were the chosen Church of God and criticised the official Church making known instances of greed and corruption. The solemnity and order in the communities were under threat although the Cathars and their religion promoted non-violence.

They are surprisingly attractive these Cathars: their lack of hierarchy, their single ceremony, their translation of sacred texts and their love of peace fascinate the modern mind. They cannot abide suffering and reject all violence in order to transcend the materiel world which is evil; they believed that they were the true Church of God. They were vegetarians, like the early Christians, they fasted often and believed in re-incarnation. Their only important ceremony was their simple baptism given at time of death with the laying of hands. They affirmed that knowledge is acquired

97

directly from the spiritual world, they translated the religious texts to be accessed directly, they did not accept the authority of the Pope and they recognized the equality of women.

"As regards the individual nature, woman is defective and misbegotten, for the active power of the male seeds tends to the reproduction of a perfect likeliness in the masculine sex while the production of woman comes from defect in the active power"

Thomas Aquinas (1225-1274) was thus expressing, in pseudo-rational terms, a universal truth of the time. But the Cathars were different: the equality of women created a gentler approach, a more liberal society and therefore a happier one. These tender concepts spread throughout the lands with courtly tunes and poems of love sung by the troubadours. This idea of gentle love is still with us.

The Cathars sound ultra-modern and most of their ideas are now part of our lives. Some beliefs have been appropriated by the Reformation while the equality of women is a progress of the twentieth century in some parts of the world. They were gentle and virtuous these Cathars; they were the flower people of medieval times; their rejection of violence made them the ultimate pacifists.

The Church of Rome was by the 12th century a solid, well established Institution; the fear of being overtaken by a small local religion seemed unlikely but Catharism was too extreme, too distant from the official Church of Rome and too dangerous for a conflict not to erupt.

In Catharism the inclusion of dualism and the rejection of the Incarnation of Christ were two concepts abnormal enough in the eyes of Christians to make the accusation of heresy an inevitable response. The Cathars were immediately represented as ungodly and therefore monstrous. The idea of a single God was well established and not negotiable and Christianity rested on the assumption that Christ - a man- was the son of God.

The Cathars central beliefs, although they though of themselves as Christians, were anything but Christian as understood by the official Church.

There were several differences the most extreme were:

1. Dualism
2. The re-incarnation of Christ.

Some less important ideas for the doctrine but significant because of their impact on the masse of believers were:

3. The clarity of Catharism,

4. The resurgence of Zoroastre beliefs,

5. And translations.

1. Dualism.

In opposition to all that is holy the Cathars believed in two gods of equal status: the God of goodness and the God of evil. The two gods were in control of separate worlds: the God of Goodness was the spiritual God, a God of love who was a pure spirit in charge of order and peace. It is the God of all that is good and the perfection to strive towards.

The God of evil is the God of the material world, all that is material and corporeal is evil, the earth and all material things are evil, the earth is a prison of matter and the God of evil reigns over the earth and all that is material. Earth is hell.

2. The Christian re-incarnation.

The second major belief which distinguished the Cathars from the Church of Rome's dogma was their rejection of the Christian re-incarnation.

The Cathars' beliefs were based on a partial recognition of Christ but because all things material were evil the Incarnation of Jesus, the son of God becoming flesh, left Jesus as a man with the taint of the material world. Jesus, the son of God, born from the womb of a woman was part flesh and therefore, to a degree, belonged to the world of matter which is evil.

Not to recognise Christ as the Messiah and the son of God is to deny Christianity, it was to be un-Christian. There was no possible concession to be made by the Cathars, the separation between good and evil is indissoluble; all that was material belonged to the kingdom of evil and therefore Jesus in the flesh was, to a certain extent, under the influence of the God of evil. With the firm beliefs that all matter was evil the incarnation of Christ, the man being the son of God was out of the question; a God made flesh was not tolerable to the Cathars.

Christianity was in the same position as there was no compromise possible to the belief that Christ was the son of God. Jesus was the Messiah because he was both the son of God and a man. The theory which rejected the godliness of Christ was totally offensive to any Christians. The two sides could not meet.

The concepts of dualism and re-incarnation were shocking enough but the other minor impediments, even though more accessible, were also truly inacceptable.

3. Catharism versus Catholicism.

The Cathars' dogma was simplistic; the dogma defined the principles of good and evil in clear separate concepts easy to grasp, a clarity which made Catharism easy to understand because it had none of the inconsistencies of Christianity. The Catholics were true Christians because they believe in the divinity of Christ while the Cathars did not.

Catholicism is complex; the Christian God is powerful and judges to give punishment or reward; evil is on earth with injustices and misery and in the afterlife with hell. God is venerated because he loves humanity enough to give his only son to be sacrificed but God punishes too and is to be feared. God is an ambiguous divinity in Christianity. Christians believe in the resurrection of Christ which is the symbol and promise of their own resurrection but they have to go through the Last Day of Judgement before their resurrection can take place. Christianity demands a judgment at the gates of St Peter since the faithful cannot enter the kingdom of God before being judged and divided between the saved and the condemned, the good and the bad.

In contrast the lucidity of Catharism had an immediate effect on the parishioners because it was easy to understand and joyful to follow. In the Cathars doctrine everything corresponded: God was good and saved; evil existed but was contained on earth. Injustice and criminals were taken care of with re-incarnation: a non-violent punishment.

The Cathars were asked to behave in a sober, pious and peaceful ways, their Bonshommes were guides who did not get rich; there were no ceremonies and no hierarchy in the priesthood; they had no need for judgment since the God of Love was ultimately successful. The Cathars were automatically saved by their Good God. This blissful concept was the basis of their attraction to the Catholics of the time and an important point to remember to understand the attitude of the Cathars when confronted by the demands of the Church of Rome. The Cathars dogma was un-demanding; it had none of the inconsistencies of Christianity.

4. Zoroastre.

The last problem was the ghost of Zoroastre, relegated as a myth the great philosopher suddenly reappeared as a mentor to the Cathars. His influence was immense and a determinant factor in the formation of Catharism. Zoroastre a religious leader, who in six hundred years BC, roughly at the same time as the emergence of the single God concept in the eastern world was still immersed in the dualist religion of the time, affirmed that the God of Goodness would be triumphant in the end. The God of love, the spiritual God would eventually be conquering all: a belief taken on by the Cathars. This joyful belief was so detrimental to Christianity that Zoroastre was denigrated, his name forgotten and his religious conviction slandered.

5. Translations.

Another attractive factor which makes Catharism different from Christianity was the desire for openness that it strived towards. The translation of sacred texts would have appealed to the more intellectual and to those who found, at last, themselves in control of their beliefs. In Christianity the translation of the Bible and other sacred texts was forbidden and did not happen before the Reformation.

The Cathars were sometimes called "Perfect"; the sarcastic Catholics who recognised their gentleness but were sceptical of their idealistic beliefs used this name for them.

The word Cathar is a title given to them later by those who mocked them; the word comes from the Greek word Khataros which signifies purified or pure.

The Cathars' Bonshommes or venerated people followed an ascetic discipline renouncing the world to attain perfection; they abandoned all materialistic goods and made vows of chastity but the believers were not expected to follow the same demanding code of behaviour.

It was not much fun to be a Cathar, it was to be sober, temperate and abstemious of all material things but in spite of the physical restraints on their lives they grew in numbers and became an extreme threat to the Christian Church of the 12th century. The Cathars must have been infuriating in the extreme and a festering boil for the Official Church. Nevertheless the reaction of the Vatican was over the top. Imperative reasons were at play to engender the quarrel but the vicious campaign which ensued was bewildering.

The Vatican is located in Italy the centre of culture and trade at the time; knowledge of the rest of the world was available; Marco Polo (1254- 1324) was back from his travel. Italy was linked to the Languedoc by the Mediterranean Sea with bustling harbours bringing merchandise, news and knowledge from all over the world. Other faiths were known and not set upon by Christianity; they were left in peace, why not the Cathars?

Although the differences between Christianity and Catharism were huge and explained the anxiety of the Church of Rome it did not explain the destructive, brutal reactions of the Vatican and it certainly does not explain the success of Catharism or the action of the Cathars at their death.

There are no doubts that the intolerant momentum to get rid of all Cathars, to destroy their writings and obliterate their faith came from the top: from the Popes themselves with the Vatican behind them. The Cathar Wars were effectively a faith-cleansing exercise which was fully successful because the culture around Catharism disappeared completely. At the time no process was found for understanding the other side's position: the Christian crowds, and particularly the priests, rejoiced in front of the pyres because at last the souls of the miscreants were saved for eternity and the Cathars faithful were elated to gain paradise for eternity.

Cathars were ordinary, decent people who did not have a chance.

On the ground the quarrel was brutal, there was no possible reconciliation; on one side the denying of the unique God was abhorrent and on the other a mysterious factor gave enough courage to the Cathars to face the almighty Church of Rome and most of Europe.

The Church reigned and was absolute master, to be challenged was intolerable. The conflict was foreseeable. The Pope called the Inquisition and from that time those who were caught and accused of heresy were burned at the stakes.

The Cathars did not survive the crusades against them but the idea was in fact academic since their faith, which was what made them Cathars, did not survive.

They were completely annihilated during more than a century of wars and Inquisition and only a few ruins of their abandoned strongholds remain to remind us of their short passage on earth.

Today the grip of the Catholic Church has lessened and the Cathars' ideas can be discussed again without danger. Christians kept the goodies of Christianity that the Cathars had to loose when they changed their faith. The Cathars were leaving behind a large amount of impressive, beneficial assets when becoming Cathars. They may have acquired a more simple doctrine and a gentler way of life but they were not only renouncing the protection of the Church and its promise of Salvation they were also dropping the opportunity to participate in the extraordinary spectacles that the churches provided. They would miss the services and would never enter the buildings full of majesty and beautiful decorations and paintings. The Cathar society may have been more kind but it did not offer the magic of the Catholic establishments with the gold and precious cloths, incenses, beautiful windows and the complicated and haunting music which transported the followers in a haven of splendour, magic and mystery and gave hope against the monsters outside. In Albi the pillars painted with brilliant colours, the dramatic paintings and sculptures added a wealth of new sensations to overwhelm the simple parishioners.

But the Cathars were prepared to discard these luxuries to belong to a religion that made their physical life more difficult. What they gained is not explained so far; to become Cathars and reject so much that Christianity could offer is still puzzling. The Cathars were popular and well like by their neighbours for their simplicity and peacefulness but they were different.

Their lives appear joyless and grim; to be Cathars demanded a lot of conviction since all physical pleasures were evil including sexual acts. Of course the Catholics were also strongly told that physical love was only for procreation, a concept that has been part of the Western culture for as long as the Church of Rome has had a say in the matter but at least they could drink and be merry and have feasts if they could afford it and they could be saved by their Church.

The Cathars were also allowed to drink alcohol but they lived a more restrained life than their Christian friends. To become a Cathar when one disliked violence was understandable but to die for it in the way they did is beyond comprehension. The life of the Cathar was close to that of saints; continuous self-disciplined and abstemious, restrained material lives were their choice. Accusations of heresy were their rewards which led to excommunication and death in a horrible way.

The Cathars still decided to be loyal to their new demanding religion. Why?

Something that the Cathars really believed in and that the Church wanted suppressed is missing; a point so important that the Cathars felt it was worth dying for. It's infuriating not to know what scared the Catholic Church into vicious aggression but gave the Cathars the courage to die rather than change their new faith.

The Cathars are remembered because their behaviour is inexplicable. Their reaction when they are taken prisoners is the total acceptance of their death. It is a strange and admirable reaction at the same time.

But if you think about it, it is a silly decision. Why not belong to the official Church? They would have worshipped the same God and been Christians still. What stopped them? To jump into the flames is an upsetting decision which brings incredulity even revulsion. Why did the Cathars behave in this way?Compromises should always be possible.

Their unanimous decision to die does not seem reasonable especially when one remembers the Religious Wars which followed two and a half centuries later in England, France, Germany, the Netherlands and Belgium where Catholics became Protestants and Protestants Catholics. The Cathars had only one word to say to be spared: yes or Oc in their Occitan of the time. They never did. or very few did.

The attraction of the Cathars' religion is difficult to understand because to become Cathars and/or to remain so meant a horrible death. It is easy to appreciate why they are not forgotten after so much time.

What they believed made their death more acceptable than returning to the Church. This is astonishing, even suspicious; people are the same across time and space: they behave following the same human patterns; to act in such extreme fashion comes only if pushed by enormously important considerations. To die the way the Cathars died demands a major reason; to die painfully does not make sense unless there is a hidden agenda which makes their deaths worthwhile.

What is left of the Cathars' writings has been seriously edited by the Church and all that is significant about their death has been destroyed. No manuscript discloses what I am looking for but nevertheless I study and read long into the nights, it is easy to miss the essential.

The viciousness of the Church campaign is difficult to explain but more astonishingly there is no justification for the acceptance of the Cathars to die, en masse, the horrible death in the pyres. The treatment of the heretics continued and was very visible during many centuries after the passing of the Cathars; worryingly the Cathars did not recant, on the contrary they accepted, even ran towards their deaths. The Cathars appeared bizarre if not deluded. The question why the Cathars rejected the Church of Rome is not resolved. An acceptable solution is needed.

Chapter 6.

The forgotten belief of the Cathars.

The decision of the Cathars to oppose the Church and to die on the pyres is still unknown. What gave them the courage to do it?

The Cathars faith is a conundrum because, although most of the Cathars beliefs are well known if not complete, the men and women's behaviour is a mystery. Something important has been taken out of the manuscripts and what remains does not reveal the reason for the Cathars' stubbornness; to let themselves be burned demands a particular form of courage; to continue to be a nuisance to a solid Institution and be without fear of the horrendous death is unexpected and incomprehensible.

Since the Cathars beliefs were obviously incorrect for Christians, especially in denying the uniqueness of God, it seems strange that the Vatican did not simply let them perish in their own delusional, noxious juices. Catharism carried, within its dogma, extreme and erroneous elements which should have repealed, even disgusted, dedicated Christians.

But in spite of the Church's rejection of Catharism and in spite of the punishments for those who dared to belong to this abominable religion no new converts desisted.

Something very strange is going on here.

The violence of the Church hides a lurking problem. The incredible aggression and viciousness of the religious campaign against the Cathars and more outstandingly the behaviour of the Cathars have meant that the people of the Languedoc still remember the Cathars with wonder.

The many arguments in favour of the Church are convincing on a deep level, to think that the unique God could be challenged about his single existence is an abomination for any monotheistic believers; nevertheless a nagging feeling about the death of the Cathars lingers with all those who have heard of them.

There is also an element of panic in the Church's reaction; an element of fear appears to have fired the congregate of cardinals and filled them with rage and determination. To execute to the last a large group of non-violent people demands exceptional reasons.

The total extermination of the Cathars does not make sense unless they posed an unknown and extreme danger to Rome, a danger which is now forgotten.

What danger did the Cathars create for the Church of Rome that is not revealed today?

The extermination of the Cathars is glossed over by the Church but not forgotten. Catharism may be old and dead, the official Christian Church may have had reasons for its action but these arguments are hardly worthy when the deaths are remembered.

A long list of visible, obvious reasons for the crusades is not paralleled by a rational explanation for the Cathars' behaviour. The Church's reasons to exterminate the Cathars are not significant enough to justify the cruelty of the Inquisition or the motivation of the Cathars to throw themselves in the pyres.

There are no acceptable explanations for the aggression of the Church and no justification for the Cathars to die their horrendous death.

Something that the Cathars believed is lethal for Christianity and a Saving Grace for the Cathars. An unusual conviction, a fundamental ingredient in their faith, a piece now lost must have been present.

When on a visit to the Languedoc they are difficult to avoid the Cathars. The old province sleeping in the sun flaunts the Cathars' identity as if to make sure that the tragedy of their past is not forgotten.

The Cathars' faith is known, their heresy is discussed but what is remembered is their end. The question is always the same: why was it necessary to eliminate them with such violence? A burden of heresy and a few ruined fortresses standing forlorn on the skyline are what are left of their passing. The Cathars seem to have little to offer. Are they worth remembering?

The answer to the question brings its own question: what are the reasons for their deaths? The Cathars are remembered because they died a violent death without understandable reasons. They were exterminated to the last as if they were dangerous but as space and resources are not the answers- there were plenty of both- the danger they posed is an enigma. This mystery has stayed in the unconscious mind of the people of the Languedoc; the insistence of the Cathars to be recognised, the numerous signs of them everywhere, the unanswered questions are too challenging to be left alone and curiosity takes over.

The smallness of the Cathars' sect should not have demanded the attention of the Vatican but the Cathars were not left alone until they had disappeared.

Looking at maps of the Old Languedoc in the 9th century the most striking factor is the immense size of the territory then when compared to the Languedoc/ Roussillon of today. It was a much larger region than the modern region; it was vast and prosperous with its own culture and its own language. Its red-bricked capital: Toulouse competed with Rome and Florence. On the Mediterranean Sea the port of Sete was a busy fishing and commercial port, a centre which reached the civilized world, and a hub of cultural liveliness and diversity; there were no doubts about the economic dynamism of the region and its openness to the rest of the world. This autonomous and independent region was also a problem for the king of France especially as most of it was under the Spanish influence. The language Occitan, a dialect with much similarity with Spanish and Catalan is still spoken in this part of France.

The preliminary punishments by the Church of Rome with excommunication then the pyres must have seriously slowed the popularity of the new faith but nevertheless the Vatican did not stop its harassment.

The combination of the crusade and the Inquisition are so vicious that they go against the idea of God as a God of love or against a Church's Institution intent in saving its people. To be Christian is supposed to be caring and forgiving…but not in this instance.

West of Carcassonne, she can see the unfinished walls in the sun. She stands next to her sister and feels hope. They both look towards the town; they know their brother Basil is working hard cutting the stones. Will they be a war soon as they say?

The two girls hold hands, to become Good Christians or Cathars, as they are called now, is the right decision. What will Basil say? She will convince him because it makes sense: to be happy in the afterlife for ever is what counts.

It is just a dream but suddenly the conviction that the problem must be tackled in a different way, the realisation that different questions must be asked becomes a clear certainty.

What had the Cathars gained they could not relinquish? What were they losing by returning to the official Christian faith that they wanted to keep at all cost?

Like all believers they were absolutely convinced that their faith was the right one; they were convinced Catholics before the Cathars came so something remarkable must have made change their faith, something that has been forgotten.

They knew that they confronted a powerful Church; many had little respect for it because it was avaricious and dishonest but they needed the Church to save them. The Institution was an authoritative and controlling force with great power.

What made them change their mind and when they had done so never to abjure, never to give way to the pressures, is astonishing. One sentence in a manuscript keeps coming back, a sentence the chronicles repeat endlessly: "…they were not afraid of death". These few words might mean that the Cathars did not fear their physical death since they jumped in the pyres but, as the Cathars cannot explain themselves, their actions must be taken into serious consideration; their actions speak loudly now that heir words have been erased.

The sentence in the manuscript: "… they did not fear death…", is both perceptive and ambiguous as it hides more than it reveals because it is true that they did not seem to fear their physical death but could it mean, also, that they did not fear the death of their souls? It was,after all the obsession of the time.

With the firm belief in the message of Zoroastre that the God of Goodness will be triumphant the Cathars souls or the eternal survival of their souls did not depend on their physical death; their God of Goodness would take care of their souls.

The Cathars were more concern with their spiritual selves than their physical selves; they were the ultimate spiritual believers and they claimed loudly that they did not fear death… the death of their souls.

Only one answer makes sense and it's the only answer which validates all the reasons for their death.

The Cathars baptism, a simple lying of hands, allowed them to reach the realm of light which they sought. It came at the time of death and opened the doors to the kingdom of the God of Love. As Zoroastre had taught, so many years, before the God of Evil is conquered just at the time of death and the God of Goodness is triumphant. Only paradise remains in the after-life. The Cathars did not expect much from their life on earth, earth is the kingdom of evil and therefore life on earth is hell.

Literally hell is on earth.

They put all their hopes and beliefs in the afterlife. Life on earth is a short passage before the reward of the afterlife. The dedicated Bonshommes meditated and re-enforced the message of this spiritual journey; suffering disappears after the baptism and the entrance into the light was guarantied.

The Catholic's dogma, like Catharism, assures the resurrection in the afterlife but there is a major difference: the Cathars' resurrection has no hell while Christians have to go through the Day of Judgement. The Cathars' God of Goodness is triumphant and therefore the afterlife is only paradise: "no hell". Hell is on earth where evil reigns, paradise is in the afterlife.

The "no hell" concept is the only explanation which makes sense of both the behaviour of the Cathars and the fear of the Vatican.

No hell in the afterlife for the Cathars.

The Cathars' religion is a hymn to the resurrection of the soul with its afterlife and acquired paradise.

Unfortunately the rejection of hell had the immediate consequence that they were doomed without hell and damned with it. To change their faith and become Catholics again was to accept the idea of hell in the afterlife. The concept of hell and suffering was against all their pacifist tendencies; torture, flames and horrors of pain for eternity was unconceivable; they believed absolutely in their rebirth and their reuniting together with their loved ones in the garden of heaven, an elated belief. But if they became Catholics then the prospect of hell in the afterlife was a reality. Their new faith brought incredible joy: no hell, no eternal damnation. God is Love.

The church was heavy on sins then. Today it is difficult to imagine the anguish of people who believed in hell, it was a reality they could not escape and purgatory was not reassuring, just not eternal.

In our sceptical modern world we understand hell as a state rather than a place, but whatever its definition hell is suffering. Hell gave fear… a lot of fear.

To ever believe that hell did not exist was a jump outside reality and knowledge because it repulsed the common sense that the reality of life imposed. Hell was real and imminent unless something was done to stop one going there.

The afterlife was a guarantee from God and an unavoidable simple truth and the afterlife was both heaven and hell. The Cathars believed the opposite, they were …abnormal.

Salvation, in the afterlife, came only with the help of the Church for Christians; only the Church could stop the terrifying descent into hell. For this reason scared people obeyed the Church. The logic behind the beliefs was unbreakable…

… except for the Cathars.

Those who became Cathars had jump out of this circle of faith and did not fear and did not obey.

Once taken prisoners the Cathars found themselves in an impossible situation: it was a choice between the flames immediately followed by an eternity of bliss or a change of faith which re-established the risk of hell for eternity. They really had no choice; to contemplate a God capable of sending its creation to be tortured in hell was an absolute impossibility because they were allergic to violence. Only a God of love and therefore only heaven made sense; they could not renounce their promised heaven.

And so they were exterminated without mercy. Their actions prove that their physical death was not a problem. To die was to discard their physical body; it really meant that they did not fear to lose their bodies since the result of their death on earth gave them paradise for eternity. The promise of paradise made bearable their short life on earth and transformed their religion into a waiting time until the guaranteed reward of eternity.After their simple baptism they threw themselves into the flames in many places. Bare feet in the dewy field below their fortress they held hands and sung; they probably took herbs and potions on their last moments to lower their threshold of pain; reality needed to be less sharp. The ordeal of the flames was unfortunate and a challenge but not ultimately crucial, paradise was on the other side and after their baptism and feeling elated they saw the God of Love on the other side of the flames.In Montsegur the field underneath the castle is still called the "Prat des cramats"…or the place of the Burnt Ones.

The Catholic Church demanded the death of their bodies to save their souls but the Cathars did not need the Church, their souls were already saved; they were going together to heaven where delights awaited them.

Hell is on earth with evil, there is only paradise in the afterlife for the Cathars.

The Cathars' religion caused deep-felt rejoicing in a physical life made bearable by the knowledge that the end would be glorious.

Up till now the statement that the Cathars did not believe in hell was just an opinion but irrevocable evidence has turned this opinion into a fact. The Cathars did not believe in hell.

Re-incarnation.

The Church of Rome was thorough; men, women and children were killed, the writings destroyed and the secret forgotten.The Cathars were neither naïve nor mislead or deluded.

They had one final problem to address and their solution took them further away from the Catholics than ever. Since all Cathars ended up in heaven Justice was not delivered.

Injustices or evil deeds were taken care of with re-incarnation. To be re-incarnated is to have failed since heaven is not obtained. To start again in this life of misery on earth was a real punishment since the reward of bliss was postponed. This non-violent punishment, for those who had committed atrocious crimes, had the advantage of suiting the gentle beliefs of the Cathars as well as giving the reprobates a second chance to start anew in different circumstances and redeem themselves.

Re-incarnation solved the problem of misconduct and law-breaking and left a God of Goodness untouched by evil. In fact Re-incarnation was logical and consolidated the belief in non-violence; unlike their contempory the Cathars did not need tortures to solve the problem of crimes.

The Cathars can be accused of being big-hearted in not wanting to torture their enemies and unrealistic in believing that criminals could change but it did not make them criminals needing to be exterminated.

The whole Cathars' dogma is simple and sensible, the Cathars were free of suffering without hell in the long afterlife; they were the "Flower people" of the 12th century. They lived with joy.

They must have been infuriating in the extreme and a festering boil for the Official Church.

Unfortunately their faith made the Cathars horrifyingly inflexible; their tragedy was partly due to their lack of doubts since it prevented conversions even if it allowed them to die with dignity.

For the Holy See the Cathars faith was a time-bomb capable of creating a revolution; it had to be extinguished, at all cost, like a bright light attracting too many moths. The Cathars appear as a sad, mislead group manipulated by forces they did not understand but a successful disinformation campaign by the Church of Rome ensured that the image of sinners and heretics endured and since none were left to refute this perception it has remained.

After the Cathars' rebellion the Church was careful to forbid any kind of mutiny and the Church of Rome reigned without major disturbance until the Reformation.

The Catholic Church maintained its hold on part of the religious Western world after the end of the Religious Wars... until now the 21st century when public opinion demands justifications.

The brutal death of the Cathars at the hands of the Christian Church was a taboo subject now re-opened. The violence of the Cathars' death reaffirms the magnitude of their secret. This brutal war was intentionally a ferocious and cruel one made even more despicable by the addition of the vicious Inquisition.

If you are in doubt about the importance of the "no hell" concept then the reaction of the Church towards the Cathars is enough to confirm that the Cathars were a serious threat.

The Cathars lived in happiness. On the face of it good luck to them, they loved God, their God was Love and they did not believe in hell; they had the best of all beliefs.

Initially it is not easy to be convinced of the Cathars' significance but the anguish of the Church, its determined need to get rid of them are signs that the Cathars heralded major problems for Christianity. The Cathars' secret is dangerous enough to convulse monotheism as we know it.

The Cathars were the first to realise the irrationality of the Christian's dogma since Christianity cannot exist without hell.

The secret of the Cathars is a rational conclusion to what happened to them a long time ago; once revealed it cannot be dismissed…

...but to know what Catharism was and to accept its secret is to enter a world in which Christianity looses credibility.

The consequences of the Cathars' secret are catastrophic for monotheism.

Chapter 7.
The Consequences.

The concept of "no hell" is loaded although it does not appear particularly interesting to start with.A negation put in front of a well-known word usually unlocks alternative views and can open untried doors but here the idea of "no hell" goes further and exposes what is going to be the beginning of a revolution. The "no hell" concept, while being the key to Catharism, violates one of the most fundamental premises of monotheistic religions.

The concept of hell and its opposite "no hell" are not simply reverse ideas they are each, in their own terms, the keys to the two religions clashing in the 10th century because hell is an intrinsic part of Christianity and "no hell" is the rallying call of the Cathars. At the same time, while being the most important factor in Catharism, "no hell" violates one of the fundamental premises of monotheistic religions. The concept of "no hell" is loaded and a catastrophe for Christianity.

The idea of hell is in the foundation of monotheism. Judaism, Christianity and Islam were at the heart of the cultures it colonised and are still in place today; the religions pervades our modern thinking and influences laws and education and shapes the religious habits of millions of people.

Hell is a fundamental base of Christianity and Islam and a reality which cannot be denied. Hell is as authentic as the fact that women give birth and as necessary as the air we breath. Hell is. Astonishingly it has never been questioned until the Cathars did and after they disappeared, the "no hell" concept disappeared with them and hell regained its power. They called themselves "Good Christians", a bizarre decision which greatly annoyed the Church of Rome but it has to be said the Cathars were hardly Christians. Theyhad, in fact, created a new religion in denying the uniqueness of a single God with their dualism and their lack of total allegiance to Christ but their rejection of hell was world-shattering in terms of monotheism.

Their rejection of hell changed a part of the dogma of Christianity and although they were genuinely unaware of the catastrophic impact of their new faith on monotheism it affected it with disastrous results.

The Vatican was infuriated but as Catharism grew and became more popular the realisation that the rejection of hell attacks the doctrine of monotheism from the inside made the Church of Rome truly anxious. The Cathars were dangerous because by taking out one of the hypotheses of the monotheistic doctrine they were in fact destroying monotheism. If one card is removed from the middle of a castle of cards the whole castle collapses; the Cathars had done the same, inadvertently it's true, but by taking out one of the premises of monotheism they were causing the collapse of thethree religions and in particular of Christianity. The idea of "no hell" is lethal.

Inherently the monotheistic religions are encapsulated in a set of premises which form a compact and cohesive doctrine which must be accepted as a whole for the system to work. The necessary hypotheses are as follows:

1. God is the only God; He is unique.

2. God is an immense power.

3. His power is perceptible in his gift of the afterlife.

4. His reward is heaven and his punishment is hell.

The three monotheist religions are based on these truths. The three distinct faiths: Judaism, Christianity and Islam, though varied, have the above four theories in common.

When punishment or hell was extracted by the Cathars from this tight list, major problems immediately followed because all the concepts of monotheism are fastened together. The monotheistic religions are unrecognisable without hell; their premises tumble down like dominos. Christianity is particularly vulnerable because the idea of Salvation is emphatically built around the Christian dogma; without hell the monotheistic religions are in danger but Christianity is destroyed.

What seemed at first the simple separation of a small sect from the official Christian Church - similar to that the Orthodox Church- it was in fact the beginning of the complete transformation of monotheism. The Cathars' break-up introduced a modification to the doctrine itself and in doing so demolished the religions.

Hell is the concrete representation of eternal damnation and eternal damnation is the consequence of the wrath of God. The wrath of God is immense because God's power is immense and limitless but where is the power of God without hell?

The "hell" concept is an integral part of the monotheistic religions; they cannot sustain themselves without it. The Vatican saw clearly that Christianity was on the brink of destruction if "no hell" became known.

Human beings are sinner from birth and therefore need to be punished or rewarded. The wrath of God is exercised with eternal damnation and eternal damnation leads straight to hell.Christianity is particularly vulnerable with the "no hell" concept because the idea of Salvation is emphatically built around the dogma.

Without hell the monotheist religions are in danger but Christianity is destroyed. To make matter worse the idea of "no hell" is simple, once explained it can be remembered easily and from there it can spread fast; the uncomplicated words leave no doubt and expand and stick. Another worry for the Vatican.

Not only is the idea simple but the first reaction in realising that the dreadful hell does not exist is one of joy. Relief washes over! Who needs hell? Another bonus added to the popularity of the "no hell" concept.

The concept of "no hell" is at the heart of the problem although it is not immediately obvious how dangerous it really is because hell is an integral part of the monotheistic religions; Christianity was seen by the

Vatican to be on the brink of destruction if the Cathars beliefs became known.

Even without examining the religious problems posed by the rejection of hell the concept of hell is irreversibly transformed if its negation is mentioned.

Hell is part of the human condition, it is the known reality of the day; it is an inescapable certainty not questioned by anybody.For the people of the 10th century "no hell", breaks this pattern. The acknowledged norm of the time has shifted from a truth to a hypothesis.

The Cathars simply saying: "we do not believe in hell" transformed hell from a reality into an opinion and in this makeover hell looses its authenticity and its power. Hell, which had been an undeniable truth, is now just an idea, even a fantasy. The certainty of hell has gone; hell is not an actuality but a fiction, a tall story, a piece of imagination and possibly even a prank. Hell is exposed and shown to be unreal and illusive.

With the Cathars, hell disappears. By not believing in hell the whole idea simply evaporates. At the beginning many Christians followed the Cathars; it's not difficult to understand why. Nonetheless hell is still with monotheism; it's a concept anchored in the dogma of the three religions and accepted by the great spiritual minds of the past and the present. Its permanence and solidity stops any questioning and makes the discovery of its irrelevance near impossible.

A simple reason explains this anomaly: to question the existence of hell is to examine the whole Christian doctrine if not the basis of the monotheistic belief.

Hell is a horrifying concept, a part of the afterlife to avoid at all cost but it has lasted a long time because it is directly linked to God. The unforeseen durability of hell is assured by God. To discuss the reality of hell, a familiar if appalling place known to everybody and which has survived for hundred of years, is to question the fairness of God or even his power.

The unexpected consequences of "no hell" shatter the very canvas of Christianity. The Cathars had not intended to arrive at such conclusions; they indisputably felt they were Christians but the law of unintended consequences reveals the reasons why the Church was so frightened.

The Christian God is complicated, it is a concept wrapped around the idea of eternal damnation, it carries with it hell and sin. Since all these concepts are closely connected they are impossible to separate.

136

To dismiss hell is to question the validity of the total idea of monotheism.

The "no hell" concept transforms the dogma in Christianity and makes the official faith look ridiculous because illogical. Do not dismiss these outrageous statements without examining them. Not only are the three main themes of the Institution of the Church, the role of Christ and the perception of God under attack but also the afterlife becomes fragile without hell if it can survive at all.

The afterlife is common to the three monotheistic religions and as such as a more profound destructive effect on the general doctrine.

Christianity is damaged by, at least, three more unsolvable problems with the "no hell":

1. It destroys the Institution of the Church,

2. It transforms the role of Christ,

3. It changes the perception of God.

The afterlife.

To start with the elusive idea of the afterlife suffers greatly without the concept of hell; its meaning is transformed from a tempting concept into a very fragile if possible idea. Three issues come to mind:

a. The afterlife needs to be confirmed: is it real?

b. Once the afterlife is accepted as an actuality the problem of its value needs to be considered,

c. And the realism of the afterlife must be looked at.

a. The afterlife needs to be confirmed: is it real?

The afterlife is both a wonderful promise and a hazy concept; in its definition it includes heaven and hell to represent reward and punishment.

One of the great assets of Christianity is the resurrection of Christ since it reinforces the authenticity of the afterlife. With this fundamental event Christianity is born and the promise of the afterlife has become a fact. That a man, Jesus, can be resurrected makes the afterlife becomes a reality. The promise of life after death is authenticated; the afterlife has been transformed from wishful thinking into reality. With the resurrection the belief in the afterlife is not a flight of fancy, it is a truth; the afterlife is now natural, possible and acceptable.

b. The value of the afterlife.

Jesus Christ having established the legitimacy of the afterlife, the resurrection nevertheless remains a fluid concept. The afterlife is balanced with heaven and hell and in Christianity it keeps its place without problems because it makes sense but the removal of hell creates an unbalance, it creates a different place. The afterlife is different and becomes a separate concept without hell. What is the afterlife without hell?

Half of the afterlife is hell. Like a coin with two sides the afterlife is heaven and hell. The afterlife without hell is an afterlife with only heaven; it is the afterlife of the Cathars, a conclusion that is only reachable if God is Love, but the God of the Old Testament is not exclusively a God of Love.

Can the afterlife survive without hell?

With an uncertain afterlife can the resurrection be legitimate?

What is the resurrection without an afterlife?

What is humanity resurrected into with an afterlife without hell? Obviously Christ will sit next to the Father in heaven but what about the sinners of earth?

Like Scylla, if one head is cut off another grows. The problems are multiple and unsolvable.

The solidity of the afterlife is under scrutiny; if half the afterlife can be discarded so easily then how safe is the other half?

If hell can be manipulated effortlessly what can happen to heaven? Is there a heaven at all? Is there an afterlife without hell?And if there is no afterlife or only a shaky one what happens to the promise of God? And if the promise of God is valueless then what is the role of God? Where is his power?What is the status of the soul, the immortal part left after death if there is nowhere for it to go?

The reward of the good Christians becomes improbable without hell. The "no hell" concept has made the afterlife into a misty, intangible concept.

c. Realism in the afterlife.

Another troublesome problem with an afterlife without hell is its lack of realism. Rightly so the Cathars were thought gullible and called "Perfect" in ridicule because their vision of the afterlife has something naïve about it; only paradise awaited them and they rejoiced in this certainty but unfortunately the lack of hell in the afterlife does not correspond to reality. The afterlife with heaven and hell is a representation of both good and evil and is modelled on the characteristics of the human condition; evil and goodness exist on earth and must therefore be reflected in the afterlife otherwise an afterlife without hell is unrealistic; it does not mirror the reality of life. An afterlife with heaven and hell makes sense; it is understandable in terms of human knowledge.

Everything on earth confirmed this balance of good and bad; humans are both good and bad; Yahweh is both good and evil; the horror stories of the Old Testament are balanced by the New Testament with its message of love and peace; the Cathars had a God of goodness and a God of evil; the afterlife has heaven - the principle of good and hell - the principle of evil, all is balanced equally. Good and evil are the two sides of the same coin; they go together. An afterlife without hell is not convincing.

The three remaining wounds inflicted on the dogma of Christianity cannot be healed either.

1. The role of the Christian Church as an Institution.

The Church's work at ground level is Salvation; the Church sees its responsibility and is emphatic on its function: outside the Church there is no Salvation. This early quote from AD 253 is the essence of what the Church is about. The strength of the Church resides in its ability to intercede with God to bring Salvation.

Salvation is the duty and the obligation of the Church, it is its "raison d'être".

Salvation in religious meaning is the saving of the soul, that is: "its deliverance from sin and its consequences". The consequence of sin is hell.

"Sin, in a strictly Christian sense of the world, takes us back to the dawn of man and the infamous apple incident" Rev. Richard Coles. Introduction to a sermon delivered in 2012.

The allusion is instant: Eve sinned: the first to do so and with her and through her all humanity will sin. God planted the tree of life, the forbidden fruit eaten by Eve.

"And the Lord commanded the man, saying, of every tree of the garden thou mayest freely eat; but not the tree of knowledge of good and evil, thou salt not eat of it…" Genesis 2:16.

"The man has become one of us, knowing and evil…" Genesis 3. 22

The importance of this obedience is so crucial that the apple incident has negative consequences for humanity. From now on humans can know right from wrong and their actions can be labelled morally good or bad because they know the difference. Eve is to blame. Eve is fundamental to the Christian's doctrine because she takes the blame for explaining why man, a creature modelled by God, can be evil. God stays perfect with the intervention of Eve.

In being able to blame Eve God is helped; he remains good and powerful and women are subdued for ages to come.

With Eve sin is born and hell is legitimate. To come up with the idea of "original sin", as Saint Augustine did, was easy; the message of God's power is left intact and the necessity of hell is firmly established. Women inferior's nature, which led to Eve disobedience, is a well known truth. From now on all humans are born sinners.

The message is clear and extremely important; the story of Eve and the apple shapesthe Christian doctrine of sin and punishment. Because of Eve humans are a sinner *in spite of God.*

The reason why humans should have no knowledge of good and evil is strange since it returns them to the state of animals, super animals of course, but animals nonetheless with no notion of right and wrong. The story of Eve only makes sense when the preservation of the power of God is taken into account. Religious scholars must have lively discussions on the problem.

On a secular level the story of Eve and the apple is based on the disobedience of Eve.

"… a woman (possibly a wife) should learn in quietness and full submission. I do not permit a woman to teach or assume authority over a man.And Adam was not deceived, it was the woman who was deceived and become a sinner". Peter.

Eve real crime is to have flaunted authority. This was a major crime in the minds of the religious male leaders who wrote the words of the bible. Christianity and in particular Catholism are based on obedience to the authority of God through the words of the Popes; Eve's crime was to doubt and to resist and with it to investigate and discover a prerogative of man.

The story of Eve is exclusive to Christianity and though monotheistic religions have common grounds other emphasis on some elements makes Christianity different.

Christianity is based on the following beliefs

1. God is powerful and fair,

2. Man is born a sinner, a fact of life

3. God punishes sin with eternal damnation, and rewards with heaven.

4. Eternal damnation leads to hell,

5. The Church saves from eternal damnation

6. Christ shows the way to redemption

7. Therefore believe and belong.

This list applies for Islam if two words are changed: Mohammed instead of Christ and Mosques instead of Church. If the concept of hell is taken out of the premises of the Christian doctrine then sin cannot be punished, going to hell is not possible and eternal damnation is meaningless, the Church and the Mosque do not save and Christ and Mohammed do not need to show the way to redemption. There is no need to belong to either Institution.

Nothing of the dogma is left except that God is the only God. Christianity and Islam are destroyed. The connections between the various concepts forms a tight logical structure; if one of these premises – like the concept of hell - is taken out the whole doctrine disintegrates.

In the monotheistic religions all the concepts are connected for the system to work. Taking one out makes the whole edifice collapses. All the premises are necessary since they only work if they are together. To interfere with one is to meddle with all.

Sin and hell are indivisible from one another, they are part of the human condition and taken for granted in Christianity and Islam.

To sin is part of the inherent nature of humans and sin conducts automatically to hell unless redemption is granted through the intercession of God, or Christ (or Mohammed) with the help of the Church (and the Mosque).

In Christianity everybody is told that they are sinners from birth, a fact easily believable as it is true that nobody is perfect; to be a sinner is the norm confirmed by common sense and the establishment of original sin. No one can be in doubt.

The Church as an Institution promises Salvation from what is the inescapable, inbuilt characteristic of being human. Like a well organised symbiotic system the believers were bound to the Institution. This tight relationship worked: the Christians of the 10th century wanted to avoid hell; they gave penances, offerings and prayers in great numbers to escape the horror of flames or flesh-eating worms, flogging, unbearable thirst, isolation and darkness and the Church saved them from this intolerable ending.

Not only was the Institution powerful in its role of saving but it could also punish the believers with excommunication and this rejection from the Church led straight to hell.

A perfect circle of need is established: the believers need the Institution as much as the Church needs them. The Church is certainly not saving humanity from criminals on earth or even the misery of life, the church is saving the soul so it can reach paradise or at least avoid hell for eternity by being purged in the purgatory, not a pleasant place but not eternal.

But without hell there is no need of Salvation, there is no need of prayers:

"Our Father in heaven...your will be done...and head us not into temptation but deliver us from evil..."

...there is no need of the Church.

The unassailable position of the Institution of the Church is shattered without hell. Suddenly the Church is deflated; its big function is discredited. What is the Church for if it does not help to save? Without hell Salvation is superfluous, a fact as valid today as it was eight hundred ago.

The Cathars were debunking hell and making the rest of the Christian population aware of it. This attack against the very foundation of the Church makes it look foolish instead of solemn. The Church needs hell to maintain its unique role.

The position of the Church becomes precarious when the saving of sinners is not needed. Without hell the priests are redundant; services, prayers, intercessions and penances have become useless, and money offerings, of course, are ended, the coffers are depleted, the rich Institution can become a pauper.

The message that deliverance can be obtained through the Church has turned into a farce. The role of the Church has become ambiguous if not non-existent.

Without hell Salvation is questionable if not completely irrelevant since without hell there is no need to be saved.

If only the Institution of the Church had been under attack and the afterlife had been the major problem the Church might have followed a different path and the

Cathars could have stayed alive but the survival of the Church is only a part of the problem and although this is a major shock for the Institution and must have distressed the Holy Father and the cardinals in dismay around him, the more generous in spirit might have accepted their own demise if the lack of hell and its consequences had only impacted on their Institution.

But it attacked the role of Christ and even the power of God. This is what engendered terror in the Vatican and led to organised massacre.

2. The Role of Christ.

Christ defines Christianity and gives his name to the religion but the dismissal of hell attacks the very centre of Christianity in attacking the role of Christ. The unique and biologically impossible achievement of the resurrection makes Christ the son of God. Christ is the only man, ever, having been seen alive after his death. In being resurrected Christ has done the humanly unachievable and therefore his appurtenance to the higher level of gods is guarantied. With the resurrection Christ is the son of God.

But the rest of humanity is not Christ and will not automatically go to heaven. Where are the souls of humanity going if there is no hell? If all souls go to heaven the need of a Saviour is obsolete; what is the point of a Saviour without a place to burn in and suffer for eternity? Jesus Christ without hell is not a Saviour; he is simply a man: a charismatic, persuasive and fascinating man but not the expected Messiah.

The implications run further since Christ becomes the son of God to be a Saviour; if he is not the Saviour since he does not need to save anybody does he need to die on the cross to be resurrected? And if he is not resurrected is he still the son of God? What is the point of being resurrected if there is nowhere to go? Is the resurrection meaningless without an afterlife? What is the meaning of the resurrection in that case?

Hell is a necessity to the dogma of Christianity. The arguments go around and around in circles; Christianity needs hell; without it the Christian's edifice crumbles and so does Islam.

The Resurrection.

An interesting if secondary sideline is the perception of the resurrection by the Cathars. They felt that the resurrection itself was ambiguous. The resurrection was not witnessed. The Cathars recognised Jesus Christ simply as a man, possibly a prophet, certainly a holy man but of course not a Saviour; but he brought the message of love which is at the centre of their beliefs and so they accepted him and thought themselves to be Christians.

Jesus is taken down from the cross probably too soon to have died; a forty-eight hour- period on the cross was the usual time before death by affixation. Jesus is taken down after twelve hours to the great surprise of Pilate who demands that the death is confirmed. Jesus is declared dead after having been checked by a centurion. A presumption? A mistake?

To be aware of deep coma rather than death was difficult then; it can be presumed that Jesus was in a coma rather than dead. The tomb is found empty the next morning by the women; it is not difficult to assume that somebody took Jesus out earlier.

In fact nobody saw the actual resurrection. Jesus was simply seen alive later. This fact was taken to mean that he was resurrected rather than to believe he might not have died.

The Cathars were aware of the uncertainties; Jesus was seen more than once apparently but his appearance to two of his followers near the town of Emmaus six weeks after his presumed death made them wonder. Which to believe: a resurrection or a recovery?

Six weeks is just enough time to heal. Why did Jesus not appear the day after his death if he had been resurrected? To appear later may confirm the magic of the resurrection but the opposite is just as believable; Jesus may have been wounded but alive when he was taken out of the tomb. The story of the resurrection is testing.

The Cathars called themselves Christian because they accepted Christ's message of love but the terrifying God of the Catholics and the flaws of the official Christian religion were not for them and reinforced the belief in their own dogma.

Christianity with the Orthodox Church, the Church of Rome and the Reformed Churches cannot survive without hell, in fact the three Brahamic religions:

Judaism, Christianity and Islam are based on a belief in the afterlife with heaven and hell.

The Cathars are extremely dangerous because in taking out the idea of hell they transform the afterlife, they destroy the institution of Christianity, they reshaped the role of Christ but they also put in question the power of God.

In Christianity hell must be part of the dogma; it is the cement which keeps everything together. The Church of Rome could not tolerate such a conclusion especially since, without hell, God itself is under attack.

3. God and Divine Justice.

The impossibility of the afterlife, the end of the Institution, and the transformation of Christ from the Saviour into a charismatic leader have inflicted fatal and incurable blows to Christianity but without hell God itself is under pressure. The popes were really frightened. God's position is diminished without hell.

The concept of God in the monotheistic religion is firmly based on its uniqueness. By having two Gods the Cathars lost the advantage of the only-God-concept which gives the monotheistic religions more power, a power ultimately bestowed on the priesthood, the Institutions and the believers. But what the Cathars had gained made it more than worthwhile to abandon this uniqueness.

The definition of God in Christianity and all monotheistic religions is that God is the creator and the ruler of the universe and source of all moral authority; the Supreme Being.

The definition given by R. Dawkins describes the God of the Old Testament as a contentious God.

"The God of the Old Testament is arguably the most unpleasant character in all fiction: jealous and proud of it, a petty, unjust, unforgiving control freak; a vindictive, bloodthirsty ethnic cleanser; a misogynistic, homophobic, racist, infanticidal, genocidal, filicidal, pestilential, megalomaniacal, sadomasochistic, capriciously malevolent bully. Those of us schooled from infancy in his ways can become desensitised to their horrors."Richard Dawkins in "The God Delusion".

The definition of God by R. Dawkins is based on the close analysis of the Old Testament and cannot be denied but it is not a complete definition because it does not include the principle of goodness which is carried within the composition of the Christian God.

The Christian God is not only a God of badness it is also a God of goodness although R. Dawkins does not acknowledge the fact.

The Cathars split this dual function of the Christian God into two separate gods. The Christian God is both good and bad and he punishes with hell and rewards with heaven.

The vision of the Cathars, although not monotheistic, is not far from the actuality of the Christian God. Their two Gods could be viewed as the two facets of the Christian God and therefore the issue of monotheism was not what made the Cathars anathema for the Vatican it was their dismissal of hell. Without hell eternal damnation is difficult; without eternal damnation the Wrath of God is pitiful; the Last Day of Judgement, so important to render God visible, cannot happen without the Wrath of God. Where is God then? God disappears without hell.

The resurrection, the sacrifice of an only son, makes God visible. Hell and the resurrection are essential concepts to give sustenance to the elusive idea of God. The resurrection is an absolute necessity to Christianity unfortunately this saving of humanity by God brings to light several problems:

a. The sacrifice of the son of God.

b. The significance of the Last Day of Judgement.

c. Justice

a. The sacrifice of the son of God.

God gave his only son in sacrifice to save humanity, but without hell what is God saving us from? God's gesture is strange and makes sense only if God, with Christ's help, can deliver humanity from hell but without hell the crucifixion becomes a straight forward sacrifice... like in the bad old days.

b. The Last day of Judgement.

God is also under attack without hell because the Last Day of Judgement has become redundant. What is the point of God as an ultimate Judge if there is no hell? God judges and sends the sinners to hell and the others to paradise. But without hell...? Eternal damnation is the reason behind hell; without hell eternal damnation is superfluous and has no meaning. Without any reason for the Last Day of Judgement God does not only lose some of his visibility but he looses also some of his power. The sending of humanity to hell by God is the one very perceptible act of God; neither his existence nor his power can be denied with the Last Day of Judgement. Abstract concepts are difficult and God is particularly elusive; his main strength resides in his antiquity and in his role in the Last Day of Judgement when he/she/it becomes noticeable. To be a Judge makes God perceptible; God literally materialises with a job needing doing; God as a judge becomes genuine and authentic. The figure of God as a Judge is invaluable to give body to the concept; a God that cannot be imagined and is at the best of time intangible is like a figment of the imagination; a God which cannot be seen, heard, touched, smelt or felt needs an action or something to make him perceptible. What is the role of God without sin and the Last Day of Judgement?

God is only defined as an idea in the mind without the Last Day of Judgement. God becomes the god-idea: more a conviction based on wishful thinking mistaken for natural instinct than an acceptable proposition. The Last Day of Judgement is essential in making God noticeable, powerful and energetic on behalf of humanity; the Last Day of Judgement needs eternal

157

damnation and hell. Without hell eternal damnation is a joke and the Last Day of Judgement meaningless.

c. Justice.

And the job is essential; God is the bringer of Justice who assures that criminals and sinners are dealt with properly, a poetic justice which balances the inequalities, miseries and injustices on earth.

But without hell there is no Justice. Justice needs heaven as well as hell.Only with hell is Justice given.

The dismissal of hell is a catastrophe for the concept of God in Christianity. Not only is God less visible without hell but he/she/it becomes powerless without hell since he cannot punish or give Justice.

Eternal damnation is essential. Without hell God is less authentic, his power is diminished. At last with eternal damnation God was visible in the Last Day of Judgement and gave Justice but without hell...?

God is superfluous without hell; an idea which impacts on the three monotheistic religions. With hell all these problems are solved; on the Last Day of Judgement Justice is re-established and harmony restored, the misery on earth is lessened with the promise of an eternal afterlife. With hell the equilibrium is re-established.

When this conclusion was reached by the Vatican sometimes between 900 and 1000 the panic must have been enormous; there was no solution except to eradicate the very existence of the Cathars and their idea of "no hell". To take the decision to exterminate these non-violent people was the only way to preserve the official Christian faith. The dualism of the Cathars was, of course, the perfect excuse to get rid of them.

Is "no hell" a supposition or a fact?

If the rejection of hell by the Cathars was a supposition to start with there is no doubt now: the evidences for their belief are undeniable; their "no hell" concept is a fact.It actually does not matter anymore if the Cathars believed in hell or not; they have left their message, now recognised and are therefore not needed anymore. The problem unsolvable in the Middle Agesis as dangerous today and as the solution applied on the Cathars is not possible now the religions are in trouble.

God has become an impossibility; the god-idea is vulnerable.

For the god-idea to become God demands faith, a great deal of faith. To believe in this invisible entity

159

supposed to rule the universe is a jump in the unknown. With Christianity the troubles do not stop there, the hurdles of virgin birth, the resurrection as well as the necessity of hell have to be overcome or accepted before the doctrine makes sense. It makes it more difficult to throw oneself into this bubble of beliefs that requires so much from the rational mind.

When the hypotheses at the root of monotheism are accepted the doctrine of Christianity falls into place and forms a reasonable religion which gives great happiness. The problems disappear only if hell exists; with it eternal damnation, heaven, the afterlife and Justice take their rightful place and God is visible.

Even so it needs a great amount of effort to integrate God. The god-idea is not innate; it must be introduced early and nurtured.

Abstract concepts are difficult and the god-idea is particularly vague and mysterious. A dedicated Institution with catechism, rituals, ceremonies and pageantry support a God surrounded by a plethora of lesser helpers: Christ the son of God, Mary the mother of the son of God, angels, Saints, apostles and martyrs as well as dedicated believers have created the image of a family, a recognisable tribe.

Religious music, stories, art, sculptures and magnificent buildings from synagogues to cathedrals and mosques have generated sets similar to the ones needed in fantasy films or science-fiction plays in which the impossible becomes believable.

Christianity is an old religion; the Emperor Constantine established religious liberty and gave Christianity its official status in 312-13 but the beliefs were started before. Enough time has passed to organise a solid and durable setting.

No real doubts are possible about the importance of the "no hell" concept. The deaths of the Cathars and the aggression of the Church are the clues not only to its existence but also to its significance.Although no documents exist to confirm the fact, nowhere is it written: "the Cathars did not believe in hell" because the Church of Rome was thorough in destroying the writings which contained this information, there is no uncertainty about it.

The Cathars rejected all compromise; they made "no hell" their rallying call. The two religions could not live together. The Vatican had no choice. It was better to strike hard immediately and kill the problem for ever rather than loose Christianity. Manipulating "the

161

people" was the trade-mark of the Institution but in this case no solutions were achievable. The joy of the Cathars was the source of their doom. The Cathars were a long time ago but Christianity is with us today. Can it survive the spread of the "no hell" concept?

The lack of hell is still a catastrophe for Christianity, it is irreparable. The problem is the same today: no Christianity or any monotheistic religions can survive without hell.

The Popes have always known. The Church's scholars had longish consultations with the Cathars lasting up to fifty years before the crusades which gave them plenty of time to work out the implications of the concept of "no hell".

The Popes still know. And keep very quiet…understandably.

Heresy is in the past but the treatment of heretics is unforgivable. The Inquisition is a crime against humanity. The intangible justification of the god-idea is not enough.

The God of the 10th century: powerful, omnipotent, mysterious and to be feared left the believers truly terrified.

What a pity the Cathars did not win their crusades! With hell gone millions of people would have lived happier lives. The Cathars are not needed anymore now that they have reminded us that hell is not a necessity; hell …can go to hell. Those who are haunted by hell must be told. Hell can vanish in a flash of thunder; hell does not need to hurt. The realisation that hell only exists for some people; that it only exists in one's mind; that it only exists if one believes in it is a welcomed relief.

No hell!

The Cathars episode, followed so soon by the Reformation, was a truly immense shock for the Church of Rome and all of Christianity.

The religion is still partly with us because of its ancient origins, because no one thinks of hell and because an immense change has taken place. The religious philosophers, thinkers, theologians, the Pope and the Vatican had been scared enough.

A solution which would take them out of the bind was necessary.

Chapter 8.
After the Cathars.

"Religion is the belief in and worship of a superhuman controlling power, especially a personal God or gods."

"Faith is the complete trust or confidence in someone or something; it is the strong belief in the doctrines of a religion based on spiritual apprehension rather than proof".

"Religions are concerned with the cause, the nature and the purpose of the universe, and many include the creation of a superhuman agency or agencies".

These definitions apply to the three monotheistic religions but the variations in each are sufficient to create dissimilar dogmas and with it different beliefs which produce distinct believers who do not always agree with each other.

In Christianity the concept of hell is central to the dogma.

Richard Dawkins' definition of God is reasonable when hell, the punishment of God, is taken into account.

What is hell?

The concept of hell is a revolting idea dreamed up by a vicious, spiteful mind who, with sadistic cleverness, thought of it as the ideal revenge. Hell is not a reality, most of the world has never heard of it. It is enough to say: "hell does not exist" for it to disappear. The non-violent Cathars could not tolerate the idea of such sadism and laughed at it.

Hell has stayed around because hell is clever; nobody is responsible, nobody can be blamed, nobody can give proofs and nobody can deny it; hell is there only if one wants it and it cannot be disproved.

In Christianity and in Islam the afterlife cannot be without hell even though nobody wants to think about it. Hell brings abject fear but to talk about paradise (with or without virgins) is to acknowledge the existence of hell.

To believe in an afterlife is to recognise hell. To believe in God in monotheist religions is to believe in hell. The soul will go back to God in a glorious afterlife of paradise or …not. To be Jewish, Christian or Muslim is to believe in hell.

It is easy to be fooled by the gentler definitions of hell that are prevalent today but they hide the fact that the only purpose of hell is to bring suffering.

Whichever way you look at it hell is bad; hell is suffering whatever forms it takes; hell has been set to produce the most pain for the longest time; hell is ache, hurt, soreness, throbbing, grief, sorrow, anguish, torture and agony all in one. Hell is continuous torment. Hell is worst than you imagine; hell is where nobody wants to be in body or mind.

Hell is not a nice place.

Paradise is all that is good and the aim of the afterlife in monotheist religions.

The Christians today are not so haunted by the fear of hell, at least outwardly, but the Muslins are terrified and will do anything to escape the possible outcome.

To believe in an afterlife is to believe in hell. This conclusion is still valid today even though it is not declared loudly or even acknowledged in Christianity. Paradise demands hell, the afterlife demands hell, to be religious demands hell and Yahweh, God and Allah demand hell. The God which can send its creation to be tortured for eternity is a God to be feared.

The Vatican was shocked by the discovery of the necessity of hell. God in Cathars' time was a scary God with the power of eternal damnation. The message had been well imparted to leave no illusion about the wrath of God and his divine power to bring Justice.

Hell is part of the culture of Christian Europe and is depicted in paintings in churches throughout the lands. In the cathedral of Albi the famous triptych of the Last Day of Judgement is a huge mural of sixteen by fifteen metres with a triumphant God between heaven and hell. It leaves an unforgettable, moving message which affects the passer-by when the understanding of the terror of the people of the time becomes obvious.

Albi is not the only reminder: The Garden of Earthly Delight, another triptych by Hieronymus Bosch (1450-1516) and the paintings by Pieter Brueghel the Elder: the Last Judgement (1558) show scenes from hell which, with obscene fascination, are familiar to all Christians.

Hell is part of our mind-set and our culture and even though it is hardly in the thought of anybody today it is still there even when not acknowledged.

The Wrath of God.

The monotheistic religions are wrapped around the idea of the Wrath of God and, in part, exist to protect hhthe

167

believers from the fury of a God who is prepared to dish out the most horrific punishment to those who are transgressing.

This statement is distressing; believers will be concerned and will try to deny it but there is no logical way out of it. Imagine a benign hell where the loss of liberty is the worse treatment and where, rather than punishments, help and advice are freely available as it should be in the best prisons of today.

Hell, with Mod-Cons and the best assistance for its inmates, is not a deterrent; this kind of hell is nothing to worry about but it's not a believable hell: it denies the very meaning and purpose of hell. It is not hell.

A benign hell affects the perception of God. A God that cannot be feared is not worth worshipping. What is the point of worshipping a God that is a good mate and gives a pat on the back and the best advice when you die? There is no need to be afraid and therefore no need to mind. For a God to be seen to be effective his punishments have to be terrible otherwise he is not worth noticing. With horrific punishments God is visible and significant. In fact the more terrible are the punishments of God the greater are his powers. The size and immensity of hell is proportional to the power of God and with it the fear which must be massive too. A gentle God is not to be feared and in that case he does not really matter.

"Unless evil is essential or necessary the religious position will collapse. Any degree or kind of unnecessary evil- however small- would tell against the existence of God as an infinitely powerful and perfectly good being". David Hume. The dialogues.

The Crucifixion.

The crucifixion is a torture and a sacrifice and sacrifices used to be offered to the gods to placate them. Everybody at the time understood the implication of a sacrifice. The story of Abraham and his son Isaac was well known.

"God said: take your only son, whom you love …sacrifice him there as a burnt offering…"

When Abraham was ready to sacrifice his son the angel of God called:

"The angel of the Lord called: …do not lay a hand on the boy…"Genesis 22. 13. and Isaac was saved.

"For God so love the world that he gave his one and only Son, that whoever believed in him shall not perish but have eternal life". John 3:16.

Gods needed to be placated with the very best that could be offered.

A sacrifice is: "... surrounding a possession as an offering to God or to a divine or supernatural figure".

Christ is the possession of God.

God surrounds his possession, his only son as an offering to ...God in order to save humanity from ...eternal damnation.

God is surrounding an offering to himself?

And eternal damnation is the result of the Wrath of God?

Something is not right here. The crucifixion to save humanity does not make sense. Could it be that Christ had to die so he could to be resurrected and be shown to be the son of God?

The sacrifice of a son is an abnormal, traumatic and enormous act so outrageous that it was forbidden for Abraham.

The problem of a God who gives the offering of his only son to placate his own wrath is strange. To exemplify how shocking hell is the most extreme sacrifice must be given; the more outrageous is the sacrifice the more terrifying hell is.

The message is clear though:the crucifixion demonstrates the love of God- maybe – but it certainly expresses the power of God.

Don't mess with God, he loves you but he can hurt and send you to hell; this seems to be what the crucifixion says. The more outrageous is the sacrifice the more God is to be feared and the more terrifying hell is.

The cross or the crucifix, which is worn around the neck of believers, is a reminder that Christ is sacrificed so that the world can be saved from eternal damnation; it is the reminder of a torture. The argument is circular and difficult to believe but if the resurrection is not a sacrifice what is it? What is the point of it? Does it prove the love of God for humanity?The crucifixion is a difficult concept.

Christianity is complex.

Christianity is puzzling and existing because some concepts in the dogma, like the crucifixion, are many-sided and complicated. There are difficult to believe.

The religion has survived for hundred of years after the end of the Cathars because the Vatican has been careful not to find itself in another similar situation as the anxious one the Cathars created.

Wary and nervous that other rebellious intelligences did not come to the same conclusion the Popes have been careful and active. Merciless measures were taken to ensure that the re-awakening of the "no hell" concept or any new ideas, which could damage the Church or lessen the religion, stayed well hidden.

Fed by this fear the horrific dealings against heretics continued, Christianity needed to be protected; it is, after all, vulnerable, the flaw that the concept of hell creates is easily discoverable by anybody who thinks outside the box. The dogma, and with it the status of Christianity, were susceptible to criticisms and were therefore in constant need of safeguard. The Cathars had violated the very essence of the religion; to let it happen again was intolerable.

The world is populated by people who do not subscribe to beliefs in monotheism and are therefore heretics according to the Catholic faith. So called heretics are left alone if they do not call themselves Christian and do not intervene with the religion.

Heretics are lapsed Christians or Christians with dangerous criticisms. Named heretics by the Vatican they do merit the most horrendous public death to punish them, shut them up and warn others.

For the Church heretics are a nuisance when they dare to oppose the Christian dogma and challenge it. The Church cannot afford to be defied on any levels. The continuous, central concern of the Church becomes a deep dread after the Cathars. Heretics have questioning minds, it is in their nature to probe and examine, to doubt and mistrust the established dogma when it does not fit with new discoveries.

The Church was all-powerful but nevertheless some did protest: Copernicus (1473-1543), Luther (1483-1546), Calvin (1509-1564), Giordano Bruno (1548-1600), Galileo (1564-1642), among a few, but they were taken care of quickly and effectively: unless they recanted or went into hiding most were burnt at the stake as heretics, as was the custom.

In fact any new discoveries were potentially threatening because they could become attacks on the doctrine of Christianity or the authority of the Church.

For nearly a thousand years the Church of Rome stopped the advancement of new ideas. The Vatican was successful in keeping intact its ancient doctrine for centuries and the Cathars became, in time, an unfortunate hiccup which had been dealt with successfully. The Cathars were gone and forgotten to the relief of the Holy Roman Church. The concept of "no hell" was dead and forgotten too. Hell as it was known could stay as it had always been.

The Reformation.

In spite of the Church's vigilance and its extreme actions against the heretics not long after the Cathars crusades the second wave of rebellion raised its head against the authority of the Popes and the Church. In 1520, two hundred years after the death of the last Cathars Martin Luther fastened his long list of protestations on the door of his church, the most public place of his town of Wittenberg.

The paper was read and approved by the dissatisfied citizens, the Reformation had started and spread fast.

To be challenged once again by a Christian movement which opposed the Pope was an unwelcome blow but the Vatican was ready: after all it had been successful two centuries earlier and although the

Reformation was unwelcomed it was seen as a small glitch which could be controlled quickly. As the momentum increased there was no hesitation from the Holy See to encourage religious fighting when the number of dissidents grew

The Reformation is a severe attack against the Church of Rome but it is not one against Christianity; it does not have the lethal effect of Catharism, it simply splits the Western Christian faith into two separate sects: the Catholics and the Protestants. Christianity was not threatened by the Reformation; only the Roman Church was in peril but the Vatican persisted with the fight, at least for a time until it finally accepted the evidence of another cessation.

The Reformed Movement was made up of people who were only "Protesting" against the corruption of the Church as well as the authority of the Popes but not against the core doctrine of Christianity. The Reformed Churches intended to stay Christian.

The realisation that the Reformation was not deadly for Catholicism but simply a spoke in its wheel meant that finally the two different but not contrary religions were left to live in peace together. The two faiths are now often represented in their respective churches side by side in the streets of the cities in the countries that had been ravaged by religious wars.

The wars finally ended and the Vatican lost its authority over a large amount of believers until eventually the two religions co-habited in more peaceful terms because the Lutheran dogma does not demolish the Christian beliefs, it simply demands more freedom of expression. What the Protestants really wanted was the freedom to revere God according to their own distinctive way of worshipping.

Unfortunately it went against the authority of the Popes who had to be jettisoned but the fundamental doctrine with Christ and God was safe.

The Religious Wars were bloody and lengthy in France, UK and a great part of Western Europe. Many died and a few changed faith: Protestants to Catholics and Catholics to Protestants.

In France the religious wars continued to rage in the 17th century till the beginning of the 18th century when the dissenting believers had been subdued, killed or made prisoners. In France the men were sent to the galleys and the women imprisoned in La Tour de Constance in Aigues Mortes. Those who had escaped abroad did not present the same danger.

It could be argued that the final outcome of the Reformation was to give a boost to Christianity and increase its popularity because it kept many believers in the bosom of the religion. The Church at that time had not sorted itself out and many believers had become disenchanted. The Reformation enlarged the circle of believers and with this greater number of dedicated Christians, who propagated their new beliefs with great zeal around the world, the popularity of Christianity was assured. The missionaries of the official Catholic religion did not lag behind in opening with great success many new churches outside Europe, particularly in South America and Africa, to the extent that now Christianity is the religion with the most adherents in the world.

In the end the Protestants, like the Cathars, wanted to remain Christian but they also wanted to maintain their own interpretation of the worship of God.

Catharism and the Reformation had specific agendas which went beyond the religious faith and was not part of the Vatican script; the Cathars wanted to get rid of hell and the Reformation wanted freedom of conscience.

Fortunately for the Church of Rome the Reformation re-confirmed the belief in hell and therefore did not carry the danger of the Cathars; the Reformation did not threaten the foundation of Christianity.

The Reformation had been a head-ache for the official Church to start with but once it was understood that the religion was not fundamentally changing the dogma of the religion the reasons for the killings disappeared.

The new danger was not perceived immediately but the Reformation is essentially the first inroad into what was to become the Age of Enlightment. The Reformed movement expended and flourished until it was finally established. It carried with it the seeds of dissent, of the questioning of authority; it showed a new vision of liberty that will later be translated into the demand for the freedom of conscience as well as freedom of thoughts, a movement fundamentally dangerous to the authority of the Popes.

The freedom of conscience.

It is near impossible to imagine the assumptions that were prevalent in the Europe of the Middle Ages until the 18th century. The air that was breathed separated humanity into two classes that were not interchangeable: the masters and the others. It changed at different times in different countries usually after horrifying turmoil; the Revolution in France and the First World War in many places in Europe were times when old assumptions were transformed.

To understand the mind-set of those times it must be remembered that the elite, those with land and status, the persons in charge of the communities, which included the religious leaders, believed that they were from a different race from the rest of the people.

The Reformation is just the beginning, soon it will be 1750 and Voltaire will publish attacks on intolerance and religious persecutions and Rousseau will state: "Man is born free..." At last the climate of ingrained prejudices was changing

The freedom of conscience is a nightmare for the Vatican because the freedom to think freely opens doors that can lead to dangerous discoveries. Once again the Vatican was terrified but it soon became clear that the Protestant Churches were intent in including hell in their beliefs; in fact some Protestant ministers ranted to extreme and although the Church of Rome had to submit itself to another bleeding of believers it was not in lethal danger of disappearing.

An intellectual rebellion similar to the Cathars' revolt the Reformation proved less deadly since many converted back and forth and the movement was finally left alone.

Freedom of thoughts is dangerous for the authority of the Vatican still intent in preserving its unique position. It's a loosing battle in our modern world in spite of the devotion of millions of believers and the insistence of the Popes that ethical behaviour is divine. The slow disintegration of papal influence in some countries continues, for example the use of condoms, contraception and abortions are current in many countries in which the separation between Church and State is not official, nevertheless the Popes deliver pronouncements and bulls on the pretext of having, as a Christian, the exclusive claim to morality. The Church of England follows the catholic dogma and like the Pope some Prelate Ministers from that Church see themselves in charge of morality and speak on matters of ethics.

In spite of the Cathars, the Reformation and the diminishing numbers in Europe Christianity is doing well in the world with Africa and South America. In fact the variety and numbers of denominations seem to increase every year.

The numbers of denominations are bewildering; now Christians are Orthodox, Catholic or Protestants.

The Protestants grew and multiplied:

Anabaptists, Anglican, Adventists, Apostolic, Baptists, Calvinists, Plymouth Brethren, Latter Day Saints, Lutherans, Methodists, Pentecostalists, Pietisms, Presbyterians and the numbers are protestantsand the numbers of sects are still growing; there are more than a hundred different ones now.

After brutish wars the Reformed congregations were left to worship on their own and divide as much as they wanted. They have added other ways of worshipping to the already numerous, different devotions of the Orthodox Churches and the Catholic Churches. Now the Orthodox, the Catholics and the Protestant religions offer three major methods of worshipping in Christianity only and these sects are themselves split into a huge variety of different factions each with their own techniques of expressing their love of God. To the Christians must be added the Jews and the Muslims who worship the same unique god.

The Christian faith is divided into sects, affiliations, factions, assemblies and congregations in thousands of diverse forms. It is not unusual to find ten different Christian Churches of different denominations close to each other in small towns in the Western World which are added to a scattering of Mosques and Synagogues to offer an amazing amount of choices to adore the single God of monotheistic religions.

The fluidity in the adoration of the single God, depicted by the three main religions each with their different sects, makes the religions perplexing.

In Christianity the continuous divisions among the Churches, in spite of the efforts of the Vatican to retain a consistent doctrine, cover the faith with a mantle of indecision. What church to belong to for monotheistic believers? There is so much choice! The demands for yet another sect seem to be coming from the ranks rather than the top as if each individual had the right to a personal view of the divine and although the Pope insists in keeping his authority - a loosing battle -God himself seems absent from this trivial pursuit. The wish of the Pope to impose his authority and keep the religion in a secure state is understandable.

Jean-Paul the Second was distressed by the continuous splits in Christianity and said:

""Division contradicts the will of Christ and is a subject of scandal in the world."

Judaism, Christianity and Islam with their infinite variations of worshipping, each enclosed in their particular devotions in conflict with the one next door, do not give confidence in the idea of a single god. The multitude of choices makes the monotheist religions appear inconsistent and uncertain.

This shifting landscape of many different faiths is complicated by the fact that Christianity, like the other two monotheistic religions, is not universal and therefore can be confronted. With modern communication the whole world is on everybody's doorstep. Other exotic philosophies and faiths are common knowledge and easily available with enough information to make comparisons. The belief in a single God is simply one of many alternatives; the uniqueness of the monotheistic belief looses its fascination.

Among the variety of philosophies, the holiness of the belief in a single God is opened to queries.

Even in the Western World, where the culture is immersed in Christian philosophy, the validity of beliefs is challenged by atheists, humanists and anti-theists.

In the East where the Islamic faith is still enveloped in a rigid authoritarian carapace the problem is not so acute …yet.

Is the God of our ancestors worth maintaining anyway?Half the world lives just as well without the god-idea so why keep it when it demands hell?

Doubts.

Established religions are being judged, an event impossible to imagine a century ago for Christianity. This creates difficult moments for the faith and doubts, more disturbing than ever, can take hold easily.

Doubts are not new; they have always been the troubled legacies of fragile dogmas. Religious doubts are distressing.

Christianity has always been riddled with ambiguities and left opened to discussions and doubts.

184

Faith is a sort of blind loyalty not based on facts; it leaves doubts to sneak around the heart of the most pious and bring anguish difficult to deal with.Doubts are the curse of faith.

The god-idea remains unproven; the existence of a powerful entity cannot be proved or disproved. This uncertainty leads to great sorrows.

Doubts are not a modern evil, even Christ on his cross exclaimed:"My God, My God, why have you forsaken Me". Palm 22.

The forthrightness of Christ who succumbed on the cross has given legitimacy to doubts.

There are many forms of doubts. A common one is the lack of understanding of God's decisions when, in perilous situations, neither compassion nor power are represented by the ultimate power. This lack of intervention seems strange. God is compassionate and powerful; his unresponsive behaviour, when it happens, is not easy to understand. "God moves in mysterious ways" is an explanation but the excuse remains puzzling. The acceptance that divine decisions cannot be questioned by a human mind is an unsatisfactory way of settling the argument.

Worries about the strength of one's faith preoccupies, coupled with the speculation that God might not be there, right beside one when he is needed, can bring anguish.

But the most dangerous doubt is the one about the very existence of God.

The Bet and Pascal.

Blaise Pascal the mathematician and philosopher in the 17th century was a man of God, a firm believer he nevertheless understood the problem of doubt. He had a response known as the "Bet". Why not believe? All could be gained if there was a God and nothing was lost if not.

Faced with the uncertainty of the existence of God, Pascal speculated:

"Belief is a wise wager. Granted that faith cannot be proved, what harm will come to you if you gamble on its truth and it proves false? If you gain, you gain all; if you lose, you lose nothing. Wager, then, without hesitation, that He exists." Blaise Pascal. 233. Pensees.

Without being aware of it Pascal's vocabulary can only come from the mouth of a deeply religious man.

The words he uses are packed with implication: "...gamble on its truth..." reveals the undeniable existence of God, God is a truth. The words: "...gain" and "...you loose nothing..." confirm heaven and with it the afterlife.

Four possible outcomes result from Pascal's words:

1. God exists and you believe that.

2. God exists and you do not believe that.

3. God does not exist and you believe that.

4. God does not exist and you do not believe that.

The first statement can be a catastrophe for believers with hell; an unappealing prospect. To believe in this Christian God bring dire punishments.

The second statement is catastrophic for none-believers; the only conclusion is their certain going to hell.

The third statement is the position of atheists and all is well.

The fourth statement is a double negation; it says that you believe in a god that does not exist. It is a catastrophe because the believer's faith ends in a void, the heartfelt beliefs are a sham. The believer believes in something that does not exist; this intellectual and emotional joke is a disaster because the believer bases all his actions, motivation and desires on the will of the wisp, on something that has no substance and no existence. This misleading belief forces the believer to behave in a childish way without independence or maturity like the very young children who believes in Santa Claus. In monotheistic religions this position carries the fear of hell.

In the end the choices are fifty/fifty. Two of the four statements are positive and two are negative and one of each belongs to the separate camps so each side is balanced. Each side has a flaw and each side has a positive ending.

In the end the contention that God exits or not forms two separate clubs; it is a personal choice that makes one jumps into one or the other. Both sides are valid equally and both are beliefs without proofs.

Pascal lived when atheism was seen as the devil's invention, he betted that to believe in God demanded little, he was right, gamblers have no hesitation.

It is worth remembering that the existence of the afterlife was not contested in Pascal's time.

Today atheists claim that the god-idea is a man-made construct and is nothing more than an invention of the mind brought in by imagination and emotion.

Their choice is as valid as the monotheistic one although the none-religious voice is new so that the equality of values on both sides is not recognised as such... yet.

The disturbing thought about the three religions is their unanimous acceptance of God and hell as an undisputed, undeniable truth. Atheism in contradiction comes from the research in depth of probabilities and the knowledge of oneself. The blind acceptance of a vision of the world given to you at birth by your parents or culture is disturbing because not personal or analysed and compared with alternatives.

The idea of God and hell are ingrained in our minds and thoroughly presupposed and seldom doubted; the premises are rarely discussed and doubts are equated with a lack of love towards God. God and hell as pillars of monotheism are inescapable truths once the jump into that club has happened. On the other side more and more evidences are coming to light that makes the god-idea more uncertain than ever. Without proof, undeniable evidences take immense strength. It is easy to be convinced.

Although horrific depictions of hell and even sermons about hell have disappeared from the modern churches it is still part of the dogma; to be a Christian is to believe in an afterlife with heaven and hell.

Hell is the prop of Christian beliefs. With it the concept of sin, which is a crime against God, and the soul which is a gift from God, make of Christianity a religion ruled by hell with its acolytes: sin and soul.

The soul is important because it entitles access to heaven. The soul is what is left after death; it is worthy of protection to gain paradise.

The soul is:

"The spiritual or immaterial part of a human being or animal regarded as being immortal."

To keep one's soul near God is to avoid hell.

These religious words: soul, sin and hell are the vocabulary of Christianity and although their meaning has seeped into everyday language the words are originally and exclusively religious. Their concepts do not exist except inside the belief in a single God. In other words atheists cannot have a soul, be sinners or go to hell.

Not to have a soul does not prevent personality, character, mind, spirit or courage. It simply means that the inexistent god cannot give anything like a soul and the inexistent soul cannot go anywhere especially since it does not exist.

Atheists cannot have a soul and cannot be sinners. They may be crooks, lawbreakers, villains, psychopaths, serial killers or mass murderers but they cannot be sinners and go to hell. They cannot go to heaven either.

For believers the memory of those who have died is present in the mind and heart of those still alive. Celebrities and all those in exalted places are remembered for a longer time; history extends their remembrance.

The belief that the soul has survived is absolute and a reason for great joy.

For non-believers the only thing left after death is the memory; for them one stays alive as long as one is remembered on earth.

Only believers in one God can be sinners; in fact Christians cannot be anything else but sinners. Which Christian can claim not to be a sinner? Saint Augustine and Thomas Aquinas made sure of that.

To believe in a single God brings the immense risk of going to hell; those who stick to one of the three monotheistic religions must live with anxiety about their future after their death on earth. The terrible punishment is defeated only with Christ and the help of the Church called sometimes the gate to heaven. The terror of hell can be avoided with an exemplary life or with the repenting of one's sins before the end.

Sins are plentiful and the wrath of God is unleashed on the Last Day of Judgement when sinners are sent to hell …or not.

The necessity for redemption and Salvation is the direct result of the belief in a powerful God who shows his power in the magnitude of his punishment.

The Protestants with Luther are not automatically sinners at birth but they get there soon enough. Calvin is even worse as he believes in predestination: the belief that one might or might not end up in hell whatever good or bad deeds have been done. Calvinists are predestined before their birth towards their final destiny of heaven or hell. The life lived can be an indication but nothing is certain until after the end. There is no fairness in Calvinism.

No wonder the Cathars decided to get rid of the Catholic God and believe in a God of Goodness!

Fortunately in the last eight centuries Christianity has changed. The exact timing is not clear but the

Christianity of today has little to do with the Christianity of a thousand years ago.

To expect a religion to last forever is to disallow its dynamism; like a living creature religions need to adapt. Christianity survives because it has changed and has become attuned to the different ideologies of different periods and today, as always, it has adjusted to modern time.

The two concepts that have been renovated are those of hell and God.

It's very clever because only their perceptions have been altered; neither of the original content of these concepts has gone from the dogma.

Chapter 9.

Transformations.

"In studying a philosopher, (here a philosophy) the right attitude is neither reverence nor contempt, but first a kind of hypothetical sympathy, until it is possible to know what it feels like to believe his theories, and only then a revival of the critical attitude, which should resemble as far as possible, the state of mind of a person abandoning opinions which he has hitherto held"

... Bertrand Russell.History of Western Philosophy.

To try to change opinions is presumptuous; to indicate different views of a subject is tolerable.

In religions transformations are not new. Already soaked in ancient tradition the old Yahweh had transformed itself and become the God of Christianity with the advent of Christ. Christianity adds to the concept of Yahweh; it does not change the premises of the monotheistic God, simply the concept of love is greatly increased. Christ gives emphasis on love, a concept already existing, in a smaller way, in Yahweh's configuration but Christ's advent marks the beginning of a revolutionary vision even if still attached to an old

194

theory; the monotheistic dogma is not changed but added to.

A new religion is born with Christianity because the change about the perception of hell has tremendous effects on the perception of God; literally a new God is born.

The God of the Old Testament, as described by Richard Dawkins in "The God Delusion" is a revolting God.

"The God of the Old Testament is arguably the most unpleasant character in all fiction: jealous and proud of it, a petty, unjust, unforgiving control freak; a vindictive, bloodthirsty ethnic cleanser; a misogynistic, homophobic, racist, infanticidal, genocidal, filicidal, pestilential, megalomaniacal, sadomasochistic, capriciously malevolent bully."

Yahweh is the God of the Old Testament; the God of Christ is different because it announces, emphatically, the importance of love with the crucifixion; Christ dies to affirm God's love for humanity, a message so important that the early Christians recognised its strength and were prepared to die in horrendous ways to preserve it.

The Christian God's concept erupted like an explosion; it was world-shattering in two different ways: it affirms the certainty of God's love and it confirms the legitimacy of the afterlife.

The crucifixion is seen as the ultimate act of love and the resurrection affirms, in the most dramatic and effective way, the inevitable existence of the afterlife.

It's no wonder that the impact of these two revelations made faith an absolute necessity and the Institution of the Church became a solid foundation.

The euphoric feelings lasted long enough to establish a world-wide religion: an incredible achievement. But fundamentally nothing had changed in the doctrine; Christianity still carried the old dogma within it.

Only the lighting is different. Yahweh is still there but he is now partly veiled leaving the new face of the Christian God in full brightness.

As years passed and the religion became a solid Institution Yahweh, who had become less prominent, reappears with a vengeance and the love of Christ, though still there, is covered by the more immediate fear of hell. The afterlife, with hell and heaven, became the obsession of the medieval Christian faith. There is no doubt that the fear of hell dominated the faithful believers and that the Church exploited that fear, to a certain extent, for increasing its power. The hysteria covered everybody including the priesthood so the intensity of the help provided was genuine because felt on a personal level by all, in or outside the Church.

The Christian God is doubled edged like the two faced Janus: Yahweh and God are stuck together and while one preserves its terrifying character the other offers a message of love. It's no wonder that the perception of this ambiguous God changes with the years. Religions are live organisms always changing so, not surprisingly, the cover of hell eventually lifted.

By the end of the 20th century another subtle change has taken place; it has slithered unnoticed and been overlooked until it explodes to leave the Christian God of today with only love in its make up; love is the nature of the Christian God prominent in the 21st century in Western Europe: God is love; nothing of Yahweh is left. God is now a God with only one face: God is only love.

The enduring image of love, which was at the heart of the extraordinary expansion of Christianity, is back on track.

But, as it was at the very beginning, old-fashioned Yahweh is still hidden behind the new mask; Yahweh lurks forgotten underneath the luminous perception of the Modern Christian God because whatever is believed the Christian God of today like the Christian God of 2000 years ago, carries Yahweh within.

The perception of the God of Modern Christianity only feels fresh and modern because it comes after the distortion which had blackened the medieval period. Like a sun shining again after the passing of a black cloud the Modern Christian God is back to the full glory of love and compassion.

But just as clearly as it was two thousand years ago nothing has been removed from the old doctrine which contains a wrathful God, eternal damnation and hell. The God of monotheistic Christianity with eternal damnation and hell exists as the same time as the superimposed God of Modern Christianity but old Yahweh cannot be seen.

The God of Modern Christianity has a huge range of multiple facets to offer from the difficult Yahweh to the total glorious, compassionate God of love; everything is there, as it was before but the light shining on one aspect only has extinguished everything else except love.

God is God, on the whole concept is stable but the idea is so ambiguous and impossible to verify that numerous variations on the same theme happen. In reality the perceptions of God fluctuate. The Christian God of this Modern Christianity is still a multi-tasking and unpredictable God: a bringer of justice, a saviour, a God who loved humanity enough to give his only son to be sacrificed but also the mean and revengeful God of the Old Testament. Yahweh is still there except that now only the face of Love is visible.

What has been transformed is the perception.

God.

The transformation may have started some times ago, it does matter when; it is fully established now: God is love.

The painful baggage of a terrifying God and a horrific hell are transformed into a God of love and a guarantied heaven. Their new formulas give Modern Christianity room to extend.

God is seen as still powerful- the definition of gods- but all compassionate. God is Love. And hell is somewhere, not forgotten but ... altered And now that

God is love the religion is flourishing in spite of the scandals. "Un souffle de vie" has been injected into it and thousand of new believers get baptised attracted by the solidity of the Catholic religion or the enthusiasm of Islam.

This new vitality seems similar to the explosion of joy felt by the early Christians. Today the lack of Romans soldiers to martyr the believers allows an unrestricted momentum.

Today the mood is similar to the years after the advent of Christ when joy motivated the conversion to Christianity.

Today the transformed perception makes the renewal of religious fervour comprehensible.

In our fast and difficult modern culture a lack of spiritual anchor is felt by some youngsters who turn towards Christianity and Islam and see them as havens of peace and authority. Life is considered safer and happier when an established belief, esteemed by the majority, respected by political leaders, newly fashionable, is easy to grasp and offers itself without strings. The promise of paradise is a strong attraction and nothing is lost by believing in it while all could be gained.

Pascal reigns again.

The awareness of Christ as a bringer of love and the new perception of hell, now seen as an unfortunate incident rather than a reality, have helped to bring invincible love in the air. Now God is love without uncertainty or hesitation.

After two millennia the old religion offers goodies with renewed success because, once again, they are tailored to the need for love.

Islam too is flourishing; many Christians convert and become Muslims in good faith while some are attracted to it, a small minority, because they see Islam as a convenient vehicle to combat Western culture.

The new perceptions in Modern Christianity are more tempting than ever because the fear of hell has disappeared.

The Christian God of two thousand years ago with its goodness and fierceness has gone, only the goodness of God is present now but of course, nothing has really been modified: the Old Testament holds true and with it, the Last Day of Judgement, eternal damnation and hell. None of this old baggage has been discarded. This Modern God of love is an effective illusion if the solid doctrine that Christianity rests on is taken into account.

Modern Christianity appears like a completely new conception of an old religion except that the old premises are still there even if hidden; a God of wrath, eternal damnation and hell are simply covered over.

As before, the premises are linked together, indissoluble and inseparable. This tight connection gives them strength; it also brings their doom because a change in the perception of one will affect a change in the others: the new perception of hell has affected the perception of eternal damnation and God.

What came first the change in the perception of hell or the change in the perception of God? The shock of the Cathars belief in "no hell" may have started the rethinking about the afterlife for the Holy fathers in the Vatican…who knows? It does not matter.

Modern Christianity.

The Modern Christianity of today would be unrecognisable to the people of the 10th century just as the Christianity of the Cathars' time is alien to us today.

But Christianity has changed successfully with subtle changes, on the surface only, delicate and understated the transformations follow the dictate of the ideology of our time. God and hell are the two concepts which have adapted and in so doing have remodelled the religion, at least externally; simply the emphasis of some aspects are so altered that it makes this Modern Christianity hardly recognisable. The old images of hell, still visible on the walls of long-standing churches, are not taken literally anymore; today they do not involve personal anxiety, they are too outlandish and therefore can be rejected without qualms. This extreme idea of hell has become historical and can be discarded as the depiction of the mind-set of people who lived a long time ago.

Modern Hell.

The hell at the time of the Cathars is without compromise, the pictures are clear: hell is a place of unbearable torture described at length by the old painters. These are depictions of the old hell. Now the changes have made hell a state rather than a place.

The old hell was visible and concrete; it is now an abstract idea, a state of mind without the power to terrorise. What is hell today?

The ludicrous hell of the Middle Ages is forgotten. The new perception of hell is sedate, from a place it is now a state of being. The fires and torments have gone; hell is now *a state of being away from God.*

Modern Christianity cannot declare that hell does not exist because it is part of the dogma of the religion but it can alter its perception of it. Hell has to stay to keep monotheism afloat but the outlandish sufferings of medieval hell are gone; hell is now a place of intellectual suffering: it is to be away from God. Just as it was for the people in the 10th century the simple solution today is to believe. The hell of today reinforces the need for believing in God.

The torments of hell are self-imposed since it only needs the belief, with all one's heart, in a God of goodness to solve the problem.

To be away from God in life is painful but can be remedied. The horrors of doubts create distressing states and are dreaded by believers. Fortunately, in life, doubts can be overcome with prayers and renewed faith and the life of the believer on earth should be a journey of devotion without worries. Doubts can bring anguish but the certainty of the goodness of God compensates from the weakness. To imagine being away from God in the afterlife must be imagined as excruciating but this state is easily overcome with renewed faith and consistent attendance to religious rituals. To believe that one's soul is not to be reunited with God is a torment but one easily assuaged since God is love and one only needs to love God back.To love God back is all it takes. Hell exists but a believer cannot really go there, God intervenes and saves. Hell does not depend on one's deeds anymore: heaven is guarantied with a God of love. There is nothing to worry about, nothing to fear. A serious believer has no problems.

Joy!

Modern Christianity, just like Catharism, brings great joy; a God of pure love, a spiritual entity similar to the Cathars' god of goodness is the Modern God of Christianity. Hell is not for believers; hell is for the others, for all those outside the faith, the ones outside the club who refuse to join; hell exists but not for believers.

And this hell has to be just as harrowing to be meaningful. Hell is for those who do not believe. Not a very compassionate idea! but I suspect that non-monotheists are not concerned.

Now Christianity offers a God who promises an afterlife with heaven and hell, a promise that is more attractive now that hell, still there, has become irrelevant.

An afterlife with just heaven is the promise of Modern Christianity. A God of infinite compassion is worthy to be worshipped.

This clever solution takes care of the problem of hell.Or does it...? Christianity is back on track. Or is it...?

The consequences of this "disappeared hell" are similar to the ones created by the Cathars: the Church Institution has lost its heart and Christ is redundant. What is the role of God?

The wrath of God, eternal damnation, the Day of Judgement and hell are myths from another time; we can live without them today.

What is left of Christianity without these concepts is a philosophy of love and an afterlife.

Wonderful!

The afterlife is a jump of faith, you believe or you don't. A rosy belief rather than a religion, a belief with nothing to fear.

It is enough to believe; the rest will be done by God. No true believer is afraid of hell today, most never think of it because it is totally immaterial; to believe in God is to go to heaven. Except that the problems faced by Christianity when Catharism appeared are back on the table. The lack of the principle of evil was compensated in Catharism by the belief in a god of evil but that is not the case with Modern Christianity; the Cathars solved the problem of Justice with re-incarnation an unacceptable concept in Christianity and without hell there is no Justice.

The Christianity of the medieval time had a powerful hell and a Yahweh still visibly nearby to represent the principle of evil without uncertainty. Eternal damnation, hell evil, the devil and an ambiguous god with an almighty wrath were balanced by the message of love given by Christ.

But today Modern Christianity has done away with any concept of evil.

Is it still Christianity?

And why is it maintaining itself so successfully?

The second question is easier to answer first. The great assets of a solid Institution prove that in spite of these problems Modern Christianity is striving; or at least appears so. It survives because it is assisted by the visible reminders of old Christianity: religious buildings, religious ceremonies, religious education, religious music, religious art, religious sculptures are everywhere and valued; they are history and culture and they keep the believers in constant recollection of the need to worship. The beauty and quantities of churches, the assumption of morality, the calendar dominated by public holidays with their vagaries of dates, the dominance of Christmas and Easter, which remain essentially religious and invade our streets and shops, are part of everybody's life. The rights of passage in church venues with spectacles and solemnity take care of the demands of daily life.

Those outside monotheism can be overwhelmed by the amount of offerings of the three monotheistic religions; the Christian presence in particular can be offensive; sometimes the loud calling of dedicated preachers on busy streets trying to gain new recruits in addition to well meaning posters proclaiming that Jesus is alive leave no doubts to the obsession of faith. In the UK the popular queen, and with it the young royal family, are seen going to church in newspaper and televisions; pronouncements from religious leaders keep us constantly reminded of the importance of Christianity in public life. A new Pope certainly gives renewed energy to Catholicism and with it monotheism.

Taken for granted, familiar in their assumption the religious, visible, outputs benefit monotheism and guarantee the authenticity of religions.

It feels as if nothing has changed. Christianity and Islam are doing well whatever the reasons for their success.

With spectacles and rituals in place Christianity attracts without the need of physical inducements or emotional blackmail. All is love; there is nothing to loose. No wonder the religion is getting more popular than ever!

It is interesting to note that, in Churches in the Western world, the mention of excommunications or eternal damnation and hell are rare except in allusions for the need to be saved. Except for some belligerent Protestant Churches, which are still raving about the wrath of God and the horror of hell, nothing is left of the terrifying Yahweh. God as Yahweh is gone.

I have found only one example of a Church in the USA which communicates the fear of hell. The minister in this Church has made a film of the horrors of hell depicted with perpetual flames and the horrific rigmaroles that go with it. Imagine the sounds of screams as well as the pictures! This film is shown to the parishioners regularly to exhort them to behave. The children are spared till they are twelve! Fortunately this is an exception: in most Christian Churches today God is only mercy and love.

But how long can it lasts?

The first question: is it still Christianity is answered by the same arguments which were valid for the Cathars. Salvation is not necessary; the Church has lost its usefulness; Christ is not a Saviour and God is diminished if not vanished completely.

The Church's job still exists, in part, since it helps the believers to stay in the right frame of mind to continue to adore God; but this ordinary role of the Institution rests on thin ice; fortunately the solidity of the Institution is still visible but for how long?

Modern Christianity.

Modern Christianity lacks what Catharism had with its dualism. Now the Modern religion has no god of evil, no reincarnation and no principle of evil. What happens to the sinners? The hell described by Bosch is gone but where is Justice. This state of infinite goodness is foreign to the reality of life. Modern Christianity has become a perfection to be reached and possessed, a dream rather than an actuality. Is it more than a world of fantasy?

Science-fiction, Tolkien, Harry Potter and digital reality open a wonderful world of fantasy similar to the story telling and oral tradition of the past. Imagination and daydream are important to detach one from difficult lives; it is soothing.

Modern Christianity helps to cope with the miseries of life; as a fantasy it is pleasing but can it be taken seriously? Can it be believed in?

Modern Christianity with a God of love and therefore without hell is more attractive than ever … on the surface but in reality it is just a little piece of fantasy. Realism and Justice are missing from Modern Christianity.

Lack of realism.

The old Christianity contains the principle of evil in the belief of hell; it is an echo of the condition of life on earth where crimes and injustices are common. This Christianity is believable because it copies the life known. Modern Christianity is only goodness. The Modern religion, devoid of nastiness with a God of love, does not ring true.

The Cathars equalized their God of goodness with a God of evil; in Judaism Yahweh is both good and evil while in the Christianity of the 10th century God was both good and bad. In Christianity God started to appear as a God of love through Christ but eternal damnation and hell maintained an outlet for the principle of evil with a busy devil. Modern Christianity has no evil; it is not realistic.

The Modern God of love is unbalanced, it does not carry the more sinister actualities of the human condition and ultimate Justice has totally disappeared.

"Evil is profoundly immoral and malevolent... force or spirit embodying or associated with the forces of the devil."

Evil certainly exists in the heart and mind of some humans but devils are like the god-idea the result of imagination.

Lack of Justice.

Without hell there is no ultimate Justice. A character in Plato's dialogues proclaimed that: "Justice is nothing more than the interest of the strongest", a definition that applies fittingly to God's Justice with the Day of Judgement; having the most clout God of old Christianity gives the final and definitive Justice. Definitions of Justice abound because they, in part, depend on cultures.

Today the following definition covers what most people would demand of justice:

"Justice is a concept of *moral* rightness based on *ethics, rationality, law, natural law, religion, equity* or fairness….the administration… takes into account the inborn rights of all human beings."

. Religions have seen themselves as exclusively able to deliver justice, an idea that still upholds Christianity but which has been shown to be faulty.

Justice does not need religions, it needs: "... to take into accounts the inborn rights of all human beings".

The Modern God.

This attractive God of love is established and not likely to be challenged because the concepts of guaranteed heaven and no effective hell are joyful tidings; the God of the Old Testament is not fashionable; who wants to believe in this revengeful God? Who thinks of hell these days and who does not equate God with love? This philosophy is wonderful. Unfortunately the old dogma has not changed with the new perceptions of God and hell. The inconvenient aspects of the dogma are not referred to but are still there. What is left is a muddle; Modern Christianity works because believers are bewitched by the idea of heaven. To know, in depth, how flawed the doctrine is, opens painful doors. Not to know allows bliss.

Now God is a nice old man, a Father who has no intention of punishing anybody.

A full circle! God is love ... just like the Cathars' God.

The Cathars had worked out the dilemma of a single God and had decided to believe in two Gods; in doing so they had clearly split the reality of the Christian God into its two inseparable principles: good and bad.

A single God presents a problem since a unique God must be both good and evil at the same time to represent reality. A single God with the principles of good and evil represents mankind; without evil God is unrealistic, even unlikely.

The ancient argument based on the existence of evil comes from Epicure's old questions which remain unanswered.

1. Is God willing to prevent evil but unwilling to do so?

Then he is not omnipotent;

2. Is God able to prevent evil but unwilling to do so?

Then he is malevolent or at least less than perfectly good;

3. If God is both willing and able to prevent evil then why is there evil in the world?

Modern Christianity seems to skip these references to evil and the power of god to intervene. The joyful realisation that the afterlife is there and is only heaven hides the reality of the human conditions. Like a light shining too strongly in their eyes the believers are blinded by the promise at the end and decide to see nothing else.

All is well, all will be well; God is there.

But when catastrophes happen what then?

This "goody-goody" state is enthralling and outlandish if not totally bizarre; it reminds me of ostriches who are supposed to bury their head in the sand at the approach of trouble.

Modern Christianity is an attractive idea; a God of love will gather his flock under his care and save all. No believers that I know have considered the possibility of going to hell; they indulge, without impediments or anxiety, in the love of God and immerse themselves in a joyful journey of love.

The angel's share is a term for the portion of wine or alcohol volume that is lost to evaporation during aging in oak barrels. The supernatural effect mellows a formally undrinkable wine or alcohol, and with some kind of magic the angel's share allows more subtle flavours to develop and special textures to emerge. The total loss varies between 2% and 14%.

What is left of the religion of the 10th century has matured and like the wines in their oak casks, Christianity has mellowed and is sweet tasting. More subtle meanings and gentle flavours have been acquired with the passing of time and the security of success. A milder Christianity has resulted; the Sunday services have been mostly silent about excommunication and the lack of pronouncement about hell is refreshing.

Nothing changes fast but these shifts in perceptions have made of Modern Christianity a belief of Love, a philosophy that is compassionate and tender. God is only love

The mellowing of the religion has given Christianity an unmistakable relevance today.

In the twentieth eighties the Catholic Church has been challenged openly for the first time in Europe. Demands for sexual honesty in the priesthood herald a new religious world where trust is part of the offered relationship between the Church and the parishioners.

In this optimistic realm of goodness the need to be saved has vanished; the selling of Indulgences stopped long ago and appear like an incongruous exercise.

The Reality of Modern Christianity.

What is left of Christianity is a philosophy not a religion. The Church services have not changed; prayers and hope are still important, rituals and ceremonies are still performed. The requirement of salvation, the prayer:

"Have mercy on us God Almighty" and "Deliver us from evil" are still used today and seem to be just as relevant.

As prayers are not aimed at the afterlife which is now guaranteed to be heaven then Salvation must be for life on earth. Redemption, deliverance from evil and salvation are demands made for life on earth.

The only problems left are the ones on earth.

There can be only one conclusion, the same that the Cathars reached: evil is on earth.

The physical and geographical evils of floods, droughts, avalanches, volcanoes erupting asteroids and any others are combined with the evil in the mind.

The demons inside one are the real devils. What is necessary is the need to be saved … on earth. Modern Christianity with a God of love eliminates the need of the Church and lessened the role of Christ. God itself becomes less visible with no Day of Judgement. In an extraordinary conclusion only the true believers are punished since they will be the ones missing being close to God.

Modern Christianity has become a psychological philosophy to help the individuals to control personal impulses from the darker side of one's personality.

One's evil instincts and deeds are the real problems. To be saved from one's own intent of negligence and thoughtlessness, of harming others and cruelty, of lack of generosity, of depression or from any crimes against others and oneself is the purpose of today's redemption.

Prayers are for the strength to combat these evils and to follow the last six of the Ten Commandments to live in a social environment without causing damaging troubles to oneself or others.

To try to remain decent in spite of miserable and unjust circumstances is worthy of achievement. Anything or anybody who helps to combat personal hells must be valued. Hell is personal and inside each one of us. To be saved is to fight against one's worse urges and unnatural, damaging and harmful inclinations in order to live a considerate life.

Life on earth is what matters.

The role of the Church and the priests has entirely changed; believers are not saved from hell; they are helped from the evils on earth. The Church gives support in time of misery but their real role has become one of psychological assistance. For that they need to be professional.

There is plenty of evil if not devils on earth; miseries, injustices, unhappiness caused by crimes, greed, dishonesty, and natural accidents are numerous and inhabit the life we live in. The problems caused on the outside are added to the problems of the mind inside oneself; we are as often the cause of our miseries.

To live is to be challenged both from the inside and the outside.

Fortunately, as social animals, we do not live alone and do not have to face everything on our own. Religious or other, anybody who comes to the rescue of others is to be remembered and praised. The affairs of earth, full of miseries from wherever they come from, need to be dealt with and given specialized help with kindness, consideration, concern, sympathy and patience as well as love. The really important point here is that expert, professional, specialized, qualified, proficient, skilled, trained help is given. The rest is icing on the cake. Fortunately services like the fire-brigade, the police, the health service as well as numerous others services have been created for no other reasons but to help and undo the harm that has happened.

To save is:

"To keep safe or rescue from harm or danger. In Christian use: to preserve a person's soul from damnation".

The second half of the definition is redundant without hell but the first half is of immense importance for all of us. The Church maintains God; it is its livelihood and purpose. Profoundly immoral and malevolent acts are committed everyday. The miseries and injustices of life intrinsic to the human condition cannot be met by just love; although love is a wonderful addition it does not solve the physical problems. Effective institutions like the Health Service, education, the police cope with crimes, miseries and injustices efficiently most of the time.

The real roles of the priests of today are as psychologists, psychiatrists, doctors, nurses and social workers, all this plethora of social, emotional and professional assistants who need to be trained in supportive knowledge to guide and help.

Synagogues, churches and mosques, with their hollow doctrines, still have the possibilities of offering secular consulting rooms, hospitals, and community centres with multiple activities for all who need it.

To have religious schools increases the possibility of conflicts. Different beliefs are dangerous when they degenerate into bigotry and create intolerance.

Modern Christianity in a new landscape of milk and honey, so far, has disguised its religious emptiness. Modern Christianity is flourishing today because a God of love is tempting.

Modern Christianity, like a chameleon changing its spots, has new colouring which covers the lizard's shape but does not change the animal. In the same way only the perceptions of concepts are different.

This confusion bewilders and keeps out of churches believers who do not find the exact reason for their disquiet but are confused enough to decide not to go to services. They say they believe in God but that they don't want to belong to the Institution of the Church; they want to follow their own personal worship. They seldom go to church, possibly only at Christmas under family pressure. Christianity both repels the more conservative believers who are perplexed by the ambiguities and attracts new adherents with its call of love.

There is no doubt that Modern Christianity is mellower; it is a philosophical system of beliefs to suit our modern time. God is love. The need for the afterlife, the strength of the soul and the promise of paradise are more in demand than ever and are still in place in today's Modern Christianity.

To add to the pleasurable impact of all these goodies the invincible problem of death, delayed with the afterlife, is still part of Modern Christianity, it attracts by its promise.

Death is a problem for us all. The hope of paradise, the promise of an afterlife diminishes the dread. This is what has made monotheism so attractive. What a waste to die? Why anyway?

The decay of the body is physical and irreducible. Death is a taboo subject because it is so painful. To accept it as part of life and talk about it might help. To rejoice in the wonder of being alive, whatever the adventures of life, might result in feeling less threatened.

I suspect that the idea of an afterlife, even a hazy one, ultimately makes death on earth more difficult to bear because the afterlife implies the possibility of a solution. If from the beginning the knowledge that life on earth is the only one death feels more natural. The religious believers expect delight and bliss after death and find life on earth contrary when they compare the two. It is not surprising to feel some resentment and annoyance when the satisfaction of justice is not always met.

That the solution of an afterlife is really impossible does not change the hope; to yearn for an afterlife is soothing. The reality, that life is death, that life and death are one, is rejected. The hope of the afterlife highlights the unfairness of life and re-enforces the impact of injustices.

To have a soul means that panic about death is alleviated; the soul takes over after death. No more panic, much less waste! After all there is an alternative in the soul! Even if the idea is absurd the relief is huge. To believe that souls can exist is a positive solution but is it worthy to believe in the unbelievable?

Both Christianity and Islam are excellent managers of emotions concerned with the promise of saving souls to gain paradise. Judaism is more concerned with the rituals of the tribe and the guarantee of its continuance. In contrast Allah has not changed in Islam where hell is very present still. The desire for paradise pushes some misguided believers into becoming suicide bombers; it could be argued that the fear of hell is the real trigger.

The wonderful advantage of the "no hell" concept of the Cathars which has triggered the changes in Christianity can only be welcomed. The end, at last, of the horrifying concept of hell will bring relief to those still haunted by the fear of hell; they can now rejoice in its demise. Those who are the Modern Christians of today can rejoice in the lack of hell if they think of it at all.

Modern Christianity can offer an acceptable philosophy concerned with the well-being of humanity…on earth! It can help the pursuit of justice on earth if it supports the State laws. Political transparency is the political calling card. Nothing except fear of their diminished influence stops the religions from sorting themselves out and putting their dogmas in order.

Our period is obsessed with love conveyed in explicit images of sex; and sex is an easy representation of feelings sometimes difficult to communicate. The Modern God is an easy God too; he/she/it makes the believer feel better now that there is nothing to fear.

The Cathars with their joyful faith had their laughter extinguished and their story ending in tears but the happy reminder that God cannot be so cruel as to send his creatures to hell can now be shouted around the Christian world without fear.

It is a great pity that the Cathars lost the war; the idea of hell could have been dismissed for ever instead of terrifying Christians for the hundreds of years to come.

Hell has been an inevitable reality and caused enough suffering in the past; it is time it went.

Now.

The Modern Christian God is the best friend you could ever have. Just love.

"God is conceived as the Supreme being, the creator and sustainers of the universe."

Maybe…

Today the God of Modern Christianity is just love.

There is nothing wrong with a philosophy of love but love is an idea, a concept.

Where is the need to worship a concept? Love is love, to be used, received and given and mostly enjoyed. But pray to it?

Love is everywhere, it surrounds us; it can be felt and used. But love is not a god.

Love is there to be plucked if wanted. Most humans need love to live; it is the survival kit of the baby; it is part of our physical life. It can move mountains.

Love is immense and wonderful. It does not matter where love comes from, to recognise and accept it is what works. This mundane love does not demand prayers; no hope is possible in the afterlife with it but the love of humans is, at last, not imaginary; real it can be experienced and enjoyed. Good luck to all those, who like the Cathars, believe in a God of love and have no hang-ups about sins or hell; at least they have love.

The ability of God to create the universe is in jeopardy with the discovery of the Big Bang and new discoveries everyday.

What is left of the old Christianity is a belief in the afterlife. To need this palliative to the horror of death and be soothed by the idea of an afterlife is a necessity for religious minds but it is a hoax for non-believers. The concept of the afterlife is an impossibility for the non-monotheistic intellect but like a sweet which appeases but does not cure and does no harm it will continue to be swallowed by those who think they need it. Except that to keep on clinging to such a fragile hope stains the integrity of logical reasoning.

Believers claim they have faith and nothing can dislodge the certainty of it. In the end one has faith or not. Those who have religion find it difficult to understand those who have not and vice-versa. The mind-sets are too far apart to meet easily.

Faith or not take your pick, both options are valid though the evidences against the god-idea are mounting and for many they are overwhelming in their reliability.

The unfortunate religious confusions are strong inducements for atheists who maintained that God is a man-made construct. Fundamentally atheists find both emotionally and intellectually the god-idea preposterous and the afterlife an imagination too far.

But a lot of people disagree.

And so in conclusion the transformations are attractive with the taming of hell and the disappearance of the wrath of God. There is nothing left of the terrifying God of our ancestors. God is love. Nobody can object but what is the point of this ineffective God?

And though heaven and therefore the afterlife are a certainty for the religiously minded it must be admitted that the possibility of their existence is small.

The final role of Christ as a messenger of love cannot be downgraded; his message of love has regained the strength it had at the beginning. Christ, whatever one believes, remains a charismatic leader, an exceptional model even when his position as son of God is questioned. The message of love given by Jesus is universal and transcends beliefs.

Love is what is left and love is what matters.

Chapter 10.

The Temptation of Love.

"Anyone who does not love does not know God, because *God is love*." 1 John 4:7-8.

"God's unfailing love for us is an objective fact affirmed over and over again in the scriptures...It originates in *the very nature of God, who is love*, and it flows to us through our union with His beloved son." Jerry Bridges. (Sometime in the 21st century.)

Religious family and friends confirm it: God is love.

God is love: these words are the mantra of today religious belief.

What do they really mean?

The two expressions demand different words because they are two different concepts.

Love is:"...an intense feeling of deep affection..."

Love is universal, available, immense and varied; it is formidable and moves mountains; it does not demand anything in return. To receive love or offer it gives pleasure. Love is an emotion which guides many actions; it grows and multiplies: the more you give the more you get.

In contrast the god-idea is not universal; half the world lives outside monotheism. God works only if one believes; God demands faith and God is still Yahweh: a vicious God and at the same time a Christian God of love. God has no compassion in the afterlife with hell. God's love is remembered because he gave his son to save humanity …from himself.

"For God so loved the world that he gave his one and only son that whoever believes in him shall not perish but have eternal life."

The idea of love in Christianity is enhanced by Christ but that love exists in combination with other elements in the nature of God so that the final image generates an ambiguous God difficult to understand.

God as only love is a modern idea. Until then the wrath of God with eternal damnation and hell made God a terrifying force that had to be coped with. Worshipping God was a form of submission to a greater and incomprehensible entity; it was also an admission of fear. The wrath of God was needed because it is the illustration of the power of God.

Now God has no wrath and does not need to be feared.

The religious writings, in particular the Ten Commandments, gave some justification for taking God seriously and for adoring him. But the Ten Commandments are a clever mix up; they cannot be accepted as totally religious. They were invaluable in helping the faith and the Institution of the Church but moral authority taken as divine for so long was in fact, as we have seen, a mistake caused by the ideology of the time.

The tricky problem of poetical justice is beautifully served by the Last Day of Judgement with heaven and hell. Justice, with rewards and punishments, gives form to the afterlife. Just these two elements: moral authority and ultimate Justice with hell make a compelling dogma even if it demands a greater amount of faith.

The association of the two concepts of God and love creates huge misunderstanding, a surprising outcome since the distinction between them is considerable. In this murky intellectual climate confusion can be maintained because love is tempting. The confusion is easily ignored for the acquisition of the benefits or the "goodies" of the religion.

A spiritual God of goodness is a perfection to look toward, a model that guides, a reassurance that life is worth living. It does not matter that the god-idea has become obscure with the many changes that modify the symbols. Anyway a God of wrath does not fit our modern society and for many the idea of love is enough. To tag God with love is expedient and gives form to the concept of God and make him a worthwhile entity.

If God offers love why not take it?

Love does not need God but the god-idea needs love. Why not just take love? The confusion is compounded because God and love are similar in some aspects, both have negative sides: love can cause extreme pain and become twisted into a negative force and God with his hell is not compassionate in the afterlife and not compassionate on earth because too often absent; the sacrifice of Christ is a debatable proof of the love of God. God's care is not consistently evident on earth where miseries are extreme for some people who face numerous injustices.

The World metre site gives statistics valid for a year. In a world of seven billion: One and a half billion do not have clean drinking water, one in six; More than

233

three million die because of contaminated water every year. More than 16,300 people died of hunger. Nearly 900 million are undernourished, one in seven.

More than one billion people are obese or overweight, one in six.

Many are born with physical or mental handicaps and haven't got a starting chance.

The Lords Prayer: "Give us this day our daily bread" is not a reality for many. The world is full of injustices, the human condition is miserable in many countries of the world

No mention has been made of mental or physical handicaps.

The most unfair deal is the time and place of one's birth. There is not much control if one is born where there is no food or born with a damaged brain or body.

The main question is always: where is this God of love when crimes are committed and the innocents are massacred? What is the point of Free Will when one's hands are tied?

The God of Christianity is not gentle in the afterlife and his concern is seldom noticeable on earth. Can he really be a God of love?

God is powerful by definition and benign in our new understanding of his nature; unfortunately these two qualities are seldom noticeable on earth where miseries and injustices are the norm too often for too many.

Some African Churches have attempted to find a solution to the conundrum. They have in mind the question of Epicure:

"If God is both willing and able to prevent evil then why is there evil in the world". God is seen as all powerful, all knowledgeable and all compassionate but there is still evil in the world an evil that cannot be generated by this God.

Something has to give.

In order to make power and compassion work together some African Churches have a solution.

Surrounded by deprivations and unfairness the devoted African Churches want to worship a God that is both powerful and caring. Their distressing solution is to believe that nasty spirits invade the most vulnerable: children and women. Exorcising these evil spirits is usually violent and can result in the death of the victim. This reprehensible practice is the direct consequence of trying to keep God powerful and compassionate. The belief in evil spirits maintains both

God's power and its goodness since this God is outside the actions of the evil spirits; injustices and miseries are not attributed to God.

The unassailable logic of this conclusion keeps power and compassion together in God, a solution that is gaining ground as more and more people seem to believe in demons; the problem is becoming serious.

God and Love are distinct, separate ideas although to interchange them is easy because there is love, there always has been some love in the make up of the Christian God. But in reality love and God are separate words and dissimilar concepts. The believer of today cannot accept a God who is not absolute goodness. If the flaws of Christianity are added to a less than considerate God the believer has to take a greater leap of faith than ever before. To believe in a God of love and ignore the faults inherent to the doctrine makes faith easier to grasp.

And we are back to faith... you believe or not.

The association of God and love is only convincing on a superficial level first because God demonstrates little love with his demand for hell. The very existence of hell demonstrates the tarnished perfection of God and the injustices on earth highlight the deficiency of a compassionate God. The love of God is conditional; God has to be believed in and worshiped before he gives his "goodies".

The uneasiness felt by believers invaded by doubts is compounded by the fact that no proof either way can be found for the existence or not of a powerful entity creator of the universe;

The speculations are numerous:

There is a God.

There is No god.

May be reincarnation?

Or anything else?

There is nothing out there

Or may be there is?

Take a coin and toss it,

All statements are correct.

Nevertheless monotheism strives and Christianity is one of the most popular among the many religions in a world of more than seven billion.

Religions, with or without god or re-incarnation, are guidelines for coping with life.

Many include formulas for feeling better.

Some people believe in many gods, some in one God and some believe in no gods at all.

The problem is that they are all correct. Everybody is right when it comes to beliefs.

The monotheistic religions are doing well but have to compete with an extraordinary array of other beliefs.

List of Religions.

Christianity is one of the many religions in a world of more than seven billion.

The monotheist religions are:

Christianity= 2.1 billion

Islam= 1.5 billion

Judaism= 14 millions.

A total of 3.6 billion people believe in a single god, an impressive number since it represents the population of half the world. Christianity is the world's biggest religion in term of numbers. Secular/ Non religious/ Agnostic/ and atheist, 1.1 billion

The others are philosophies usually without gods and others are religions with many gods.

Hinduism= 900 million

Chinese traditional religions= 394 million

Buddhism= 300 million.

Jainism, Shinto, Sikhism, Taoism and Paganism are some of the others.

There are thousands of faiths, beliefs and philosophies in the world.

Some religions: Hinduism, Jainism and Sikhism include reincarnation with the idea of rebirth. Reincarnation is the belief that the spirit or soul comes back in a different physical form after the death of the body. Buddhism is similar with re-incarnation and incorporates the veneration of Buddha.

Some religions like Hinduism have many gods.

Some like Taoism have a philosophy or recipes for emotional and spiritual survival.

Religions, with or without gods or re-incarnation, are guidelines for coping with life.

Many include formulas for feeling better.

The Premises of Christianity.

God is: "… in Christianity and other monotheistic religions the creator and ruler of the universe and source of all moral authority, the Supreme Being".

This definition does not involve emotions or love or even the idea of a carer.

In an extraordinary way and in spite of criticism and flaws in the monotheistic system monotheism is doing well.

Monotheism is like a club that you enter after having accepted a set of rules. Once these rules, or in this case a set of premises is accepted the system works as a cohesive belief.

The hypotheses are together to form a strong structure in which all the elements are linked; each ring in the chain sustains the others.

In order to gain the rewards of Christianity on earth or in the afterlife a certain number of assertions have to be accepted as facts:

1. God exists and is the creator of the universe.

2. God loves the world and has a son.

3. The son of God: Christ is a man.

4. God gave his son to save humanity.

5. The afterlife is a promise of God confirmed by the resurrection of Christ.

6. The afterlife is heaven and hell.

7. Believe in God and you will be saved from hell.

Once these seven hypotheses are taken for granted God has a certain appeal even though to go through the doors of faith demands a halt to reason.

Who wants to believe in this amass of hypotheses? How can one believed in it? Now that God is only love the religion is even more tempting but at the cost of the integrity of the mind.

The price to pay for believing in God is high; it is true that the rewards are enticing but this reaching for happiness can be too exacting since it demands the abandonment of reason.

And is happiness worth preserving at the cost of rationality?

The Happiness Parasite's Story.

The happiness parasite can only survive by clinging to a human brain but it curtails the life of its host by a great numbers of years. With the permission of the victim the parasite settles like a hat on the head of the assenting individual who has a guaranteed life of happiness and from then on the most appalling tragedies can be managed without distress. It does not take long for the whole population to accept the parasite.

The people die young with a smile on their face. There is no uncertainty in the gamble here; happiness is guaranteed; nevertheless accepting the parasite is equivalent to suicide, a slow one, it is true but fast enough to shorten the bulk of one possible life. Temptation is a cruel friend and hope, his companion, continues the impossible. Nevertheless the god-idea attracts young people who have joined the club and become dedicated Christians because they feel they have gained unconditional love and a place in paradise. The monotheistic religions require a lot of faith in their demand to believe in miracles, in impossible happenings or simply in an invisible entity and … all without proof.

An Old Man.

Faith is: "complete trust or confidence in someone or something; strong beliefs in the doctrine of a religion, based on spiritual apprehension rather than proof."

The intangible figure of God is a comfortable vessel for containing love. The popular image of an old man representing God reminds the believers of the love of a caring father. God is a difficult concept but this concrete image from the past fits as an emotional need; it is, after all, the picture of a caring father. Possibly it makes this God more appealing because the unconscious wants a guide, a mentor, a counsellor or just a vague "something more" to have a life fulfilled.

In more liberal Churches the idea of hell or even the afterlife is never mentioned. The prime goal of going to church or of being a believer is to be guided; it is to look up to the idea of a supreme force for good and to know that, with God, life has a purpose. Nothing more is needed, the beliefs, symbols, the deeper meanings can be ignored in this communal worship which makes the members of the religious community feel better.

Like the fear of hell of the medieval period this desire for the love of God is like a collective hysteria; logical reasoning is done away with for the advantage of feeling better. The pendulum has swung the whole way from abject fear to total love.

The love of God confers vast amount of love and happiness because of heaven and heaven is a temptation difficult to ignore even if it is an empty one.

The Institution of the Church, the traditions, the culture and the history of the land are behind the Christians of today; they give the strength to continue to believe in spite of doubts. Believers can believe that the earth is flat because everybody that matters to them says so. The love of God is wrapped around the assets of Christianity: the message of love given by Christ, the ancient lineage which enhances respect, the ceremonies and the rituals in use everyday and the "Good Works" all surround the god-idea and strengthen God.

To believe in the Christian God of today remains a convincing option because it envelops one in devotion and delight …as long as faith is sustained.

The idea of a personified God is essential because it sits well with the multitude of helpers which are part of the Christian story: a son: Christ, a mother: Mary, a husband: Joseph, a friend: Mary-Magdelene, apostles and disciples who all create a complex human family while angels and saints add a touch of divine to confirm God. God and Jesus his son, who is a man, are together the link between heaven and earth.

Warm feelings and yearning for security are associated with the images of this tribe; a sense of belonging and excitement reinforced by the ceremonies and rituals move hearts with universal longing. The numerous chronicles assist powerfully to fabricate a believable saga.

The Modern God is greatly enhanced by the concept of love. Love gives God legitimacy; it gives him weight and makes him perceptible. The rituals of life and death representing the essence of our human condition are illustrated by Christmas and Easter with wonderful pageantry. The crucifixion depicts the killing of the innocent and general human suffering while a complete account of the conditions of life and the nature of man in the Old Testament and the New Testament keep the believers riveted. They are so many interesting stories and ideas in the religious writings around monotheism! They have produced a gigantic block of history full of life's events that are difficult to abandon and to top it all they are viewed as divine. The trappings of religion are impressive. God is easily available and makes one happy; to think that God could be let go of is to abandon love too or at least it feels like it. Without the god-idea love seems to loose strength as well as history and culture; to abandon God is to let go of the familiar and the fascinating... or so our emotions tell us. It is like missing Princess Diana.

To adore concepts or people that cannot be accessed fully or known in detail is attractive because there are no risks. In those cases only the superficial is on show or only the viewpoints that are deemed worthy are available but the regular observation of these features render them familiar and therefore dear and valued. Who did not love the Princess and who did not think they knew her well?

It is called propaganda and it works if you believe!

Put together Christianity is impressive in this beginning of the 21st century: love, an afterlife, ultimate Justice, a Father figure, and the creator of the universe are the incentives for believing in God; beliefs packaged in ceremonies and "Good Works" the faith carries with it a welcome feel good-factor.

Independence.

To see the end of God seems intolerable. Frequent images, continuous stories, famous places, respect of exalted people keep the god-idea alive; to do away with the religious traditions is felt like a loss.

But in exchange it is to gain independence and intellectual integrity and more importantly it is to exchange an emotional view of the world for a more rational one.

In monotheistic religions the guarantees are built on wishful thinking, they rest on desire for what is imagined and for what is dreamed; fantasies are transformed into realities.

In spite of its grand offering there is no certainty and no guarantee in the afterlife or the god-idea.

No wonder doubts creep around the most religious minds!

Happiness is precious but not at the expense of lucidity.

To believe in a single God or gods is to let go of part of rationality.

Trustfulness, a kind of innocence, a fear of the future or a lack of confidence led to faith but more probably complete inertia about what was imposed at birth - imposed because there was no choice - is the answer.

The only factor that gives strength to the god-idea is its link to love, but love does not need God. The happiness given by God is valuable but love can be found outside the god-idea and be just as rewarding.

In Christianity the perception of love and the belief in a positive afterlife rest on implausibility; an afterlife which turns out to be nothing but fantasy needs to be remembered only as an historical aberration.

Monotheism is presumptuous; the inspection of its doctrines leaves many holes, doubts and flaws.

The Cathars' belief or the negation of hell is the beginning of its Nemesis…possibly.

Nemesis from the Greek mythology is a goddess usually portrayed as the agent of divine punishment for wrongdoing or presumption. It is the inescapable or implacable downfall of someone or something especially when deserved.

Nemesis is retributive justice.

The arguments which terrified the Church at the time of the Cathars have not disappeared. The Church of Rome, which has known the flaws of Christianity since the Cathars, has kept quiet because the dangers have not disappeared. An educated and dedicated Vatican knows the flaws of Christianity but will never be prepared to admit the problems. It cannot.

The demand for transparency, which is the political fashion of today, has started to invade the long corridors of the Vatican but Christianity, with its marvellous organisation and hold on half the world, can continue to preside without fear of discovery.

The lack of hell impacts on Christianity but also on Islam. Islam, a monotheistic religion at the forefront of intellectual discoveries in the Middle Ages, is now enmeshed in the necessity to use the religious laws as the laws of the land.

The fear of hell motivates suicide-bombers who die knowing they will be remembered as heroes; they expect an eternity of bliss.

For Christianity the problem of "no hell" is insoluble; there cannot be a hell with a God of love and with "no hell" the arguments valid at the time of the Cathars are back again: the Institution and purpose of the Church are gone; Christ is not a Saviour and the Last Day of Judgement is immaterial. Everything that makes Christianity has disappeared and even God is diminished.

Monotheism was based on fear and maintained by bullying. Now love has taken the place of fear. It has increased the motivation for religion even if it only works with great efforts of faith and lack of reasoning.

Fortunately love remains.

Chapter 11.

Beyond Monotheism.

In the Western world the god-idea has been soaked in this established belief for thousands of years; today it has problems but because of its many advantages it is not easy to abandon.

Humans are thinking creatures questioning and demanding answers: to live exclusively in the material world is not enough.

"The Western world has done away with religion but not with our religious impulses; we seem to need some higher purpose, some point to our lives - money and leisure, social progress, are just not enough." Jeanette Winterson in: "Why Be Happy When You Could Be Normal."

Jeanette Winterson expresses a necessity for "some higher purpose" which she equates with religious impulses.

The need for something that is not "money and leisure, social progress"; the search for something that is not wholly materialistic is the realm of religions or has been seen as such until now but a multitude of other possibilities can also fit Jeanette Winterson's words.

The spiritual may be part of us but the material is as important.

Spirituality from spiritual is: "… relating to, or affecting the human spirit or *soul* as opposed to material or physical things."

The spirit is: "… the non- physical part of a person which is the seat of emotions and character; the soul".

The seat of emotion includes feelings, sensation, passion, sensitivity, affection, concern, love, consideration, anger etc… while character consists of personality, moral fibre, courage, integrity, qualities, and individuality and more; all these are part of the spiritual in us; so is beauty, harmony and peace for example and all these characteristics are features of all of us.

The insertion of the word *soul* in the definitions of the spirit and the spiritual immediately pushes these words into the realm of the afterlife and therefore religion. Jeanette Winterson's comment about "religious impulses" being part of human nature: …"we seem to need some higher purpose…" With these words she indicates that humans cannot live with only the material world.

The implication that religious impulses lead to "…higher purposes…" integrates the spiritual with religiosity and is the direct result of the dominance of monotheism in the culture it has touched and it implies that only the religious can be spiritual. To want this "higher purpose" goes beyond the material but to have longing for the spiritual does not have to be resolved by divine intervention. The god-idea is not a necessity in the concept of spirituality. The spiritual emphasis of religions with the soul and the afterlife, which are at the heart of monotheism, exaggerates the need, even creates the desire for a "divine". But as we have seen the god-idea is fragile if not totally based on imagination. The spiritual in gods, God, the devil, demons and angels leave more to fantasy than reality. Spirituality can be found outside the religious in spite of the fact that materialism has acquired a negative connotation in our societies, a feeling promulgated by religions, so that, now to be labelled spiritual is usually understood to mean involved or interested in the religious.

Materialistic is "…a tendency to consider material possession and physical comfort as more important than spiritual values."

"More important" are the crucial words; to be materialistic is a question of degree. Most individuals, religious or not, are both materialistic and spiritual. The most spiritual believers in terms of religious beliefs have been the Cathars.

To be spiritual without being religious is to put thoughts and emotions, rationality and thoughtfulness above one's personal comfort. We are all spiritual but we are not all religious.

Without God.

To live without the god-idea pauses problems especially for the religiously minded. Beyond queries about the creation they worry about life on earth and have the following questions in mind:

1 Why live?

2. How to live?

3. How to cope with the miseries of life?

Without God the answers are less easy but solutions are available.

The ones devised by Camus are interesting. As an atheist he found personal answers and wrote novels to explain his philosophical thoughts. He was sent to Le

Chambon sur Lignon, a village in the Cevennes which had a difficult time during the religious wars and had an extraordinary destiny during the 2nd World War. Camus was sent there for his health where he wrote the beginning of "La Peste. In the following summers, faithful to the place, he came back staying in different hamlets around the village.

I regret that, too young, I never saw him. His view of human destiny without the god-idea resonates with genuine and rightful sense.

I imagine him, smoking his pipe, thinking and walking head down in the streets of the village preparing the pages to write in the evening by a warm fire.

Human nature requires answers but they do not have to rely on an uncertain entity outside of ourselves.

1. Why live?

Monotheism is successful because it provides many goodies; it is comforting. To be born, to suffer then to die seem meaningless. Gods give answers.

Camus, like most people in the Western world today, was privileged because he lived at a time and in a place where the freedom of conscience and the freedom of thoughts were taken for granted. It is not a given right and women in Taliban-controlled countries, for example, have a hard time preserving their intellectual integrity. We cannot boast of our liberality since religious thinking was heavily dominated by monotheism until well into the 20th century. To go to the synagogue, the church or the mosque on a regular basis was expected. The laws of the Church still prevailed in Europe till well into the sixties where the number of adoptions at birth of babies born outside wedlock was the direct consequences of the Christian Church's rule. Not to be a member of one of the monotheistic religions was not an option.

Camus thinks outside the religious box.

In "The Mythe of Sisyphus" -1942 – he examines the reasons to live. In "L'Etranger" -1942 he looks at what life demands. In "La Peste" he examines pestilences or everything that brings suffering.

Never dictatorial he simply explores ideas and communicates them.

Le Mythe de Sisyphe.

What is the meaning of life without the god-idea? "In a world devoid of religious unity or values man's search for meaning becomes a passion."

The search for meaning was Camus' passion in life. His first question: is life worth living for its own sake is answered in the "Mythe of Sisyphus".

Sisyphus, a king in Greek Mythology is punished for being deceitful; he is made to live a meaningless life. He pushes an immense boulder up the slope to see it fall down again ad infinitum. It is the most useless, physically demanding, boring and undignified job possible. Why should Sisyphus not end it all? Does he? Sisyphus does not kill himself but goes on living.

"The Mythe the Sisyphus" is an argument against suicide. Like the mountain which is climbed because it's there Camus affirms that life is there and must be accepted and lived. The mountain does not have to be climbed but life must be lived. Camus is uncompromising: there is only one choice: to live like Sisyphus. "You live because you have a life. Life is there for you, live it".

The arguments to convince that life is worth living are fragile; the first one is awareness. Sisyphus is a man who struggles to live and this struggle makes him aware of life.

"The struggle itself towards the summits is enough to fill a man's heart."

Because he knows he has a life Sisyphus becomes a man in control; he is a man responsible for his life. He recognizes that he has a hard life and in doing so he becomes in charge of his destiny.

He accepts and … decides to live. The greatness of life is to be alive. The struggles to stay alive is what makes staying alive an obligation. In doing so Sisyphus finds his place and his purpose.

Sisyphus is not unhappy with his pushing of rocks because he is a man who controls his fate by controlling himself. Awareness, knowledge, acceptance of the raw deal makes him a man. He struggles; he accepts; he does the job and he lives. With this understanding he gains a sort of cheerful satisfaction and dignity. The struggle is enough.

"One must imagine Sisyphus happy" is Camus' conclusion.

Camus' deduction seems complex compared to the religious rule which forbids suicide in monotheism. To kill oneself is a crime against God and therefore a sin. The punishment in Christianity is going straight to hell. The Church shows its rejection by not allowing burial in consecrated grounds.

The religious demands are possibly more persuasive but they deny independence and control of one's life; to live rests on obedience to an order from God while, for Camus, the necessity to live springs from knowledge and acceptance of life. The joy is in being alive, knowing it and surviving. The struggle itself is enough.

Life is for living but up to a point, this assumption is as naïve as is the religious command against suicide. A dreadful circumstance or a depressed mind can lead to the compulsion to take one's own life. Unfortunately we pay a high price for our thinking minds and regrettably religions are not an impediment to suicide. Suicides are not uncommon whatever the beliefs.

Camus finishes "The Mythe of Sisyphus with a quote from Oedipus: "I conclude that all is well".

"L'etranger"

Camus was thinking of "The Mythe of Sisyphus" and "L'Etranger" at the same time since the essay and the book were published in the same year. "L'Etranger" is the natural continuation of "The Mythe de Sisyphe".

The obligation to live that concludes "The Mythe of Sisyphus" is acquired in

"L'etranger".

The title of: "L'Etranger" is awkward; the book is sometimes translated as: "The Stranger" but better named as "The outsider". In "L'Etranger" Camus answers one of the question which surrounds the idea of an accepted life or how to deal with life.

Camus describes a man who is the opposite of Sisyphus. Meursault seems to be an anti-hero, a puzzling, strange man with no feelings and no real need for people.

"I opened myself to the gentle indifference of the universe."

Meursault eats, sleeps, has a girl-friend and exists in a sort of physical life with no other purpose than survival. He lives without either happiness or misery. He is insensitive and unperceptive; occurrences happen to him by chance; he is not the master of his actions; in other words he is not a man aware or a man in control of his life. He is as opposite to Sisyphus as possible. Meursault is a being without the power of emotional or spiritual thoughts at least before his trial.

Meursault goes to his mother's funeral, that is what is done but he does not understand why, he feels no regrets, no love, no unhappiness.

"Mother died today. Or maybe yesterday; I can't be sure."

Meursault is physical; he copes with the material world and finds significance only on that level. He does not love anybody or care about anything.

"I explained to him, however, that my nature was such that my physical needs often got in the way of my feelings."

Meursault is dependant on events not in charge of them as illustrated with the pointless murder; Meursault does not choose a path; he tumbles where the next step takes him and reacts to the immediacy of the situation.

"His glaring fault in the eyes of society- he seems to lack the basic emotions and reactions (including hypocrisy) that are required of him. He observes the facts of life, death, and sex from the outside…"

Meursault eventually kills a man one day on a beach, a man he has never seen before. He kills without knowing why he killed. When asked he replies that the sun shone in his eye, the reflection surprised him.

Meursault is judged and sentenced to death. When the priest visits him he refuses to see him. "I had only a little time left and I didn't want to waste it on God.

"… Even when involved in a personal tragedy he (Meursault) considers his own feelings and the reactions of others with a calm and almost ironic truthfulness." Cyril Connolly.

Meursault has turned his life into a pointless emptiness; he lives his life like a foreigner in his own land; he is an outsider to his own life.

"There is not love of life without despair about life."

Camus is emphatic about the difficulties of life; "…there always be rats".

What matters is how one copes. Difficulties and death are part of life.

Camus has a habit of killing the characters he does not approve of; he kills Meursault possibly because Meursault's indifferent behaviour is an insult to life.

"L'etranger" is a difficult, many faceted book.

When he had finished it Camus wrote the following lines:

"My dear, In the midst of hate, I found there was, *within me*, an invincible love. In the midst of tears, I found there was, *within me*, an invincible smile. In the midst of chaos, I found there was, *within me*, an invincible calm. I realized, through it all, that... In the midst of winter, I found there was, *within me*, an invincible summer. And that makes me happy. For it says that no matter how hard the world pushes against me, *within me*, there's something stronger – something better, pushing right back. Truly yours, Albert Camus".

This quote is the voice of Camus expressing his love of life, his pleasure in the thrill of being alive, of the greatness of being able to breath and wait for tomorrow. Inner self gives great strength. Camus' poem is an hymn to life.

And it is what Meursault could not see and be.

Camus is an existentialist; he believes that philosophical thinking started with humans. To refuse the marvellous offering of life from nature and have the power to think is to reject living like a human being.

Camus' ideas are not always easy. "A struggle towards the summits" which ultimately bring happiness because of control is the theme of: "The Mythe of Sisyphus".The need to live with passion even if it brings pain is the concept behind: "L'Etranger". Is it enough of an incentive towards life? It is a beginning. Camus gives both meaning and happiness to the process of living. Life can be a passion which gives contentment and purpose. In that context the god-idea is not a necessity; a passion for life is enough, a passion for life which feeds on itself and becomes enthusiasm and dedication.

"You will never be happy if you continue to search for what happiness consists of."

"But what is happiness except the simple harmony between a man and the life he leads."

Numerous interpretations and different analysis about "L'etranger" abound. Camus is not a judge or a proselytiser; he comments on what he observes (like Montaigne with his Essays). Camus indicates directions and unlike the Christian Church does not suggest that it is the only path; Camus simply proposes other options, other choices than religious ones.

Camus is opposed to the religious tradition, particularly the Christian one of keeping knowledge away from the people. Knowledge brings power over others and Christianity was emphatically opposed to communicating knowledge. Personal knowledge brings personal control.

Knowledge, understanding, comprehension and communication are all important to Camus. In "L'etranger" he recounts how Meursault finds, in a discarded newspaper, the dramatic consequences of lack of communication. Camus wrote a play based on the story called: "The Misunderstanding" to underline the necessity of communicating knowledge. Catholicism has demanded blind obedience and still does; this authority stops the thinking process. Knowledge has been the bane of Christianity. The Popes have been frightened of the discovery of the flaws in the dogma.

Islam was at the forefront of scientific advancements in the 6 to 10th centuries with its development in mathematics, its understanding of medicine and its control of irrigation in desert lands. It had marvellous libraries to rival with the one in Alexandria destroyed in 47/48 BC with the incalculable loss of countless manuscripts (a library has been rebuilt now on its old site next to the palace of Cleopatra covered by the Mediterranean Sea).The Islamic libraries were equal in their acquisition of priceless scrolls and knowledge; the numerous scholars kept the civilisation of the world from sinking into an age of darkness and ignorance.

Today, in some Muslims areas, the learning by rote of passages of the Koran without understanding the meaning of it because in a different language from the one known, has made a sad farce of this exceptional intellectual movement that was at the heart of the Muslim communities.

It is a disturbing practice for those outside the circle of that particular faith because it associates a certain kind of meaningless piety with education. Can the knowing by heart of the Koran assure a place in paradise?

In Christianity: "Eve and the apple story" is a controversial account since it denies to Adam and Eve the knowledge of good and evil. It is probably no more than a religious puzzle necessary to make humans capable of being evil; it has the great advantage of leaving God with his goodness and his power, evil has nothing to do with the divine.

Women's status has been inexistent for thousand of years because the bible crystallised what was the general belief in a society controlled by men. The same is happening today in some part of the Muslim world where the conviction in the inferiority of women continues, an absurdity that has become a truth which is re-enforced by the interpretation of some pages of holy books and the ideology of the culture. It seems that reading and learning the Koran or the getting of any kind of education is only allowed to males. In some countries, Islam appears as dark, backward and prejudiced as Christianity was in the Middle Ages.

More importantly obedience destroyed the importance of information, a move that suits religious authorities; lack of information leads to easier control of the population; knowledge is power. Eve is the heroine of the modern area and the curse of the Christian tradition because she dared to investigate. Her curiosity is seen as doom. Unfortunately there is no Eve in the Koran. A few extreme believers, like the Taliban and other extremists who belong to Islam, represent only a very small number of the total allegiance to the religion; unfortunately, like all trouble makers, they are more noticeable than their numerous and peaceful religious companions.

La Peste.

Camus liked le Chambon, a place which had been riddled by religious conflicts. It must have tickled his humorous buds to be an atheist there!

To live is to struggle. Life is a challenge filled with suffering and death.

Camus in "La Peste" examines what he calls pestilences: pestilences bring suffering.

The day to day details of living with disasters and malice, suffering and pestilences, is the theme of "La Peste".

Camus was writing at the end of the Second World War, a period when questions about the horrors of life were in everybody's mind and heart.

Questions about the: "why life" are difficult and universal. Why there is evil is partly answered for believers when they trust in God.

For non- believers this religious answer is not acceptable. Without God the answer must come *from within oneself* as Camus suggests and as the two previous questions of "why live" and "how to live" are answered.

The plague is the pestilence chosen by Camus to investigate the impact of disasters on an ordinary community; he examines the reaction of people when disaster strikes.

What to do in the face of suffering? Is there a way?

"La Peste" tells the story of the town of Oran on the cost of North Africa invaded by dying rats; it is the start of an epidemic of plague that will keep, for many weeks, its stronghold on the town. The plague is a pestilence, a disaster and a symbol for human suffering.

Camus uses the reactions of his characters to express the different ways people cope with pestilences. The first reaction is disbelief soon followed by fear. Some inhabitants declare that the plague has nothing to do with them and close their doors. Not to want to see the pestilences does not mean that suffering does not exist.

Soon people die.

Many of the inhabitants try to escape and leave the town before the gates are closed; a fair number decide to help in the crowded hospitals.

Camus includes more personal characters; the bad guy uses the situation for his own benefit and becomes a wealthy smuggler imitating the collaborators during the war. A cynical father becomes involved in the rescue of the plague-victims only after his son's death. Being affected directly prompts to action.

The good guy Grand is the quiet hero; his symbolic name gives him away:

"He was one of those rare people… who have the courage of their good feelings… his personal life vouched for acts of kindness and a capacity for affection which no one in our time dares to own to."

Many inhabitants are victims of the disease and suffer and die.

Pestilences are not just suffering coming from the outside, they are part of ourselves too: "…each of us has the plague within him; no one, no one on earth is free from it".

In the second part of the book Camus develops what is the most horrifying for him: child suffering:

"… nothing on earth was more important than a child suffering…a child suffering… the horror it inspired in us….these innocent victims had always seemed … to be in fact what it was: an abominable thing".

The child who dies suffers horribly during long days of pain. The priest Panellou, the representative of the Church and therefore religions, a gentle man cries when the child dies. The priest is moved and ultimately destroyed by the death of the innocent because he cannot find the answer to the question: where is the compassionate God he believes in? Is God incapable or unwilling to save the child? The priest dies of a broken heart.

Before the child died the priest had told his congregation:

"…calamity has come on you my brethren, and you my brethren, you deserve it…" a statement so horrifying that Camus rejects this medieval interpretation without hesitation:

"No Father. I have a different idea of love. And until my dying day I shall refuse to love a creation in which children are put to torture".

The priest is a kind man moved by the death of the child who he tries to understand his God. To make sense of what has been his whole life he says:

"But perhaps we should love what we cannot understand"…the easiest course was to surrender … divine compassion would do the rest".

But Camus cannot accept the priest's position and declares:

"Who would dare to assert that eternal happiness could compensate for a single moment of human suffering?"

"… and among things evil he included human suffering".

Camus was writing seventy years ago but in 2009 the sermon from a bishop maintained that New Orleans had been flooded during the terrible storm of 2006 as a punishment from the Almighty because the town had not rejected its gay population. A few days after the statement the Pope reinstated to his full religious functions this controversial man of God.

Nothing has really changed in the religious realm.

To cope with pestilences is never easy and heroism is not for everybody. But Camus insists with his moderate advice, moderate only in appearance since it is not easy to execute: to simply fight against pestilences is demanding.

"Why! that is not difficult! Plague is here and we have got to make a stand; that is obvious … it is up to us, so far as possible, not to join forces with the pestilences".

Rats and pestilences, suffering and misery are part of life. To deal with suffering is not easy and Camus' answer seems mild: "Not to join forces".

A simple statement difficult to fulfil.

Camus repeats it several times:

"…the only means of fighting the plague …consists in doing my job".

The doctor, the teller of the story continues to try to cure and save the people of the town says:

"…doing my job… to take a stand…one must do what one can…" He is the voice of Camus.

"I only know that one must do what one can to cease being plague-stricken, and that's the only way in which we can hope for some peace."

"To do what one can" against pestilences.

Not to accept suffering of any kind but to fight against it the best one can is Camus' answer.

At first sight this obvious and mild advice does not appear too demanding but it implies a huge commitment. Not to ignore pestilences, to work against them can lead to dangerous situations. The doctor and those who helped against the plague were putting themselves in danger of catching the terrible illness. The Resistants during the war when caught were tortured or killed. To go against pestilences, to fight against them brings risk.

To be against pestilences and do something about them is a strong advice not a simple or easy decision.

Camus believes that man is in control of his life; the individual aware and responsible makes his/her decisions. Each one has the task of giving a meaning to his/her life. Life is a challenge and a struggle; to do the best possible with what it throws at one is the only way. Passion and happiness are the rewards of mature humans who are aware, responsible and in charge.

Camus acknowledged the difficulties of life, it is a struggle but he had a *"liking"* for humanity; he liked the idea of life and the people who make up humanity.

This quote from a man who had just witnessed the 2nd World war was:

"A man who was sick and tired of the world he lived in though he had a liking for his

fellow-men" defines Camus who makes a distinction between circumstances and people, between pestilences and people coping with them.

Camus is a realist, disasters are part of life.

He finishes the book when the plague has disappeared with a warning: plagues are never far away or done away with for ever…

" …as he listened to the cries of joy rising from the town, the doctor remembered that such joy is always imperilled… the plague… never disappears for good… and that perhaps the day would come when, for the bane and the enlightening of men, it roused up its rats again and sent them forth to die in a happy city."

Pestilences or suffering will always be there; they are part of life.

There will always be rats.

Camus is also remembered for what he called: "The philosophy of the Absurd" which is not part of the Existentialism movement. Camus was born in 1913 in Algiers in North Africa; he died in France in a car accident in 1960.

Negative aspects of monotheism.

Camus offers a different vision, a set of concepts that preserves individual dignity while offering guide lines. This philosophy has the advantage of presenting less negative consequences than monotheism.

Monotheism:

1. Brings conflicts.

2. Is built on lies.

3. Has a confusing numbers of outlets.

4. Uses natural instincts to reinforce its message

5. And misinformation has brought twisted perceptions.

1. Religions Bring Conflicts

The three monotheistic religions have been at the roots of numerous conflicts throughout the ages. In Christianity the Cathars, the Inquisition and the religious wars were horrors and between Christianity and Islam the crusades were dreadful; the Jews suffered an inhuman holocaust seventy years ago and were persecuted throughout the ages. Unfortunately the relationship between the three religions is still not free of clashes.

Some aspects of religions are not forces for good; divergence of thinking brings conflicts. Horrendous quarrels from yesterday are still prevalent today.

Religious beliefs harden concepts and transform them into personal causes needing to be defended.

The past insistence on the universality of the Catholic faith and the use of missionaries (Protestants were there too) have imposed new behaviours on communities around the world not always for the better.

The Catholic Church has not yet put its house in order in regard to its priesthood and sexual assaults.

Major unhappiness is being created by its condemnation of contraception and safe sex with the advice of avoiding condoms. Provocations for emotional reactions against gay marriages are not helpful.

Morality is another area which brings conflicts since religious establisments still insist on their hold on ethic from flawed grounds. Morality is not restricted to Christianity in spite of its conviction. Atheism lies outside the influence of God's will, modern States are not controlled by the authority of the Church; they do not need religions to find reasonable solutions to their legislative problems. Islam has not discarded its religiosity to administer its legislation…yet.

2. Christianity is built on lies

The difficulties in the dogma of Christianity cannot be overcome because a belief in hell is a necessity in the doctrine; without hell the afterlife is inexistent and monotheism becomes fragile.

Without hell the structure collapses and with hell God is not compassionate.

The deceptions crept into the beliefs, the falsehoods were not deliberate; there was no intent to deceive but these faults have been known by the Vatican for nearly a thousand years and nothing has been done.

The promise of the afterlife is an elusive concept that cannot be substantiated but it is the main pledge of Christianity.

The hope in a positive afterlife is the desire of believers.

"Hope is a feeling of expectation and desire for a certain thing to happen."

And the afterlife is a desire not a certainty or even a reality; it is a hope based on uncertainties and wishful thinking. Such a flimsy basis for a belief is similar to an untruth, even a lie.

"The bigger the lie, the easier it is for people to believe it".

"A lie repeated ten times remains a lie, repeated ten thousand times it becomes a truth"

"When a lie has been sufficiently repeated to the point of being common knowledge of the truth, the more enormous it is the more difficult it will be to redress it."

Unfortunately these three quotes fit monotheism perfectly and explain, in part, the increase in the faith. The thin line between reality and fantasy makes illusions, mirages, fantasies, misconceptions, misunderstandings, errors, imprecision and mistakes real.

The religions have acquired a substantiated life because the desires or hopes they rest on are attractive but, in fact, their doctrine is built on immaterial will o' the wisps.

Lies are powerful but not to be tolerated when known.

It is intellectually demeaning to believe in a system that is flawed.

3. Religions have large numbers of outlets.

A confusing numbers of outlets characterise the monotheistic religions. The vast list of some of the dominations attached to Christianity is bewildering in its variety and quantity. To them must be added the other Christian faiths: the Orthodox Church and the Protestant Churches. Judaism and Islam are also part of monotheism. A list of monotheistic religions: Judaism.

Christianity which includes the Coptic Church, the Orthodox Churches, the Protestants Churches with their hundred of denominations.

Islam with Sunni and Shia and in the Shia's branch the Alawites of which President Assad of Syria is a representative; a sect which numbers 12% of believers. Atenism followers of Akhenaten who believed in the Sun-God.

The Bahai I faith.

Cao Dai. Cheondoism. Deism. Eckantar. Hinduism with Vaishnavis and Shivaism, Raviddassia. Seicho, no le, Sikhism or Sikhi with 30 millions Sikhs who believe in one God who prevails in everything; Tenrikyo and Zoroastrian.

This list does not include the hundreds or rather the thousands of denominations related to each of these main religions.

Religions, with or without god or re-incarnation, are guidelines for coping with life.

Many include formulas for feeling better.

Jean-Paul the Second was distressed by the continuous splits in Christianity and said:

""Division contradicts the will of Christ and is a subject of scandal in the world."

4. Religions use irrational impulses.

Some irrational impulses have fed monotheism and are still at the centre of it:

a. Basic instincts,

b. Talking to oneself,

c. Santa Claus.

a. Basis instincts

Subtle, insidious triggers sustain the god-idea by valorising the concepts. For example hell is felt to be real because it reflects the reality of the human condition. Miseries and injustices as well as happiness and success are on earth and therefore the afterlife, like a mirror, must parallel the conditions of earth. No conscious thoughts are involved; the afterlife is the replica of what is the reality of earth. To go beyond this instinctive afterlife with its good bit and its bad part is problematic because it is so ingrained in the culture and because it is the echo of the known reality on earth. Life on earth is both good and bad like the afterlife.

The god- idea probably evolved from the need to explain an incomprehensible, completely baffling environment; why would the mountain suddenly explode unless something very powerful had intervened?

The intuitive projection of hell rests on nothing but natural instincts; this is another reason why hell is not discussed but accepted as real because it echoes the reality of earth.

b. Talking to oneself

In the same way the habit of talking to oneself, of talking to this other self outside oneself, who gives the right answer, who is always there and is the best friend ever, is an ordinary and natural behaviour. It is called thinking. We do it continuously. Who does not talk to their other self when they are in trouble? Or ask God for advice if they are believers? Born believing in one of the monotheistic religions who does not call on God for one reason or another? It is easy to misinterpret this ordinary human act for a divine conversation.

Reactions that are natural and part of our human make-up, to the extent that we do not think about them, have been used to reinforce beliefs in God. They strengthen the concepts and give religions authenticity.

c. Santa Claus

The need to think of God as a caring father is implanted in the young child early on.

Santa Claus is a caring old man who brings presents, just like a father would! and like God he is called father!

The explosion of the Father Christmas' symbol is unstoppable because it resonates in us as a need: the desire to be taken care of.

Young children before Christmas! Delight and expectation are in their eyes. Christmas' festivities with wrapped parcels, trees, lights, music in shops, tinsel, and Father Christmas in corners of streets are unusual, they are only there for a few days so anticipation is in the air and expectations are high. The attitudes of adults who promise an unforgettable treat give the occasion profound meaning and turn the red clad figure shaking his bell into a genuine character.

Santa Claus brings happiness, who can deprive the children? There is no harm in it! The children get pleasure and excitement; the parents glow with the warm feeling of having done well and seeing their children happy.

Santa Claus has religious advantages because, from now on, the father symbol is well implanted in the mind of young ones. Father Christmas reinforces the authenticity of God the Father, a benign carer giver of goodies...

... except that Santa Claus is the neighbour next door in a funny gown. You, the perpetrator, know it is a sham; know it is a show, a fantasy, you know that none of it is real.

Father Christmas is authentic for the children; the pageantry and the parents' reactions are persuasive...

... they believe.

Later on they realise the trick, they have been duped. Regretful or cross they soon rejoice in being grown up; they even start to mock the youngsters who still believe! They feel superior and are contented; they know that they have gained the world of adults, the world that matters.

They know that they know; they have passed the first test. Father Christmas is a caprice played by adults, a bit of fun for the sake of the children, except that the idea of a caring old man who suddenly appears and brings presents is now a concept lodged for ever in one's consciousness.

Later on the child understands that God takes care of humanity, a continuation of an idea which appears plausible and is accepted without questions. The same dedication, the same spectacles and the same commitment by adults affirm the authenticity of God.

In the old days Saint Nicholas used to have a whip as well as a bag of presents; the bad children were punished just like God punishes with hell.

5. Religions manipulate perceptions.

Religions are powerful and still have an extraordinary influence on everyday lives on everybody whatever their beliefs.

The predominance of the monotheistic culture is so invasive that the lack of God feels like a calamity. The influence of the Christian religion can be felt everywhere in the Western culture. Thirty years ago in the UK religious education was the only subject that was demanded, by the law, to be taught in classes where the register asks for Christian names. In the USA, the richest and strongest country in the world, the president would not dare to admit that he was not a believer.

"No, I don't know that atheists should be considered as citizens, nor should they be considered as patriots. This is one nation under God". George HW Bush 41^{stt} President of the USA.

Surprising comment since the separation of State and Church is written in the constitution. The first amendment of 1778 asks:

"...to refrain from recognising the religion of Christianity, or one of its denominations, as an established, state church".

On one side of dollar bills; one dollar, five dollars, ten dollars, twenty dollars ... is written: "In God we trust".

The religiously minded, including some religious leaders, are opposed to gay marriage and not long ago to be homosexual was a crime punished by prison in most countries in the world. In Islamic countries it is anathema.

Religions are introduced with our mother's milk; they become embedded inside our skin. "Give me the child" said the Jesuit, "and I will give you the man" an accurate prediction. Religions are implanted and are difficult to dislodge.

Many reasons can be found for dumping monotheistic faiths but nevertheless the god-idea remains a strong contender for beliefs. If one is born in one in the religions it is difficult to see outside it.

Monotheism is successful today. Until not very long ago, those who did not adhere to monotheistic religions in the Western world, were perceived by the religious believers, particularly those in Christianity, to be lacking moral fibre, happiness and a creator.

This list of ingrained impulses helps the concept of God to stay in the mind.

a. Lacking morality.

b. Lacking happiness.

c. Lacking a creator.

a. Lack of morality.

Morality is not restricted to Christianity in spite of the conviction of monotheistic believers. To be outside the influence of God's will is not to be immoral. The State's legislation of many countries is now secular and not controlled by religious authority; secularity carries the stamp of morality. Laws are guardians of morality and the arbiter of ethics, they do not need religions.

Suitable, reasonable solutions are being found to difficult problems without religions. Morality has nothing to do with religious beliefs.

b. Lack of Happiness

There is no doubt that Christian beliefs bring happiness to those who believe but those outside the god-idea are not unhappy. For the believers to imagine the happiness of atheists is near impossible; they picture the lack of an afterlife, and with it the hope and relief they bring, as a catastrophe. In our western society atheists are seen as less happy by those who have not experienced the happiness of living without the god-idea.

The unhappiness theme is widespread; a religious disinformation campaign has made sure that afterlife and happiness are equated. It is true that with the afterlife death does not appear to be final and this brings great relief: death is not final. But the afterlife is too uncertain to be alluring for atheists.

Still the question remains: how can one be happy without God or the afterlife?

The lack of belief in a life after death seems to bring sorrow to those who hope for it.

Atheism is seen as lacking in the happiness of the afterlife, a belief easily understood.

How can atheists be happy?

In truth death is so final that anything that can alleviate this end seems worthwhile. This is monotheism's great strength. Believers are loath to abandon the idea of living forever even if the virtualisation of paradise is hazy. The idea of something else after death is what matters.

The fact that it is improbable is not a worry.

But it is possible to live with contentment without the hope of an afterlife; to know that all we have is all there is gives intensity to life.

The perception that believers do better in difficult circumstances is tenacious. Patients in hospital are supposed to improve faster than those without a faith. The perceptions enmeshed in a religious culture leave long shadows and the rumour prevails.

David Lodge in his book: "Deaf sentence" expresses the feeling of many through the words of his main character:

"I envy religious people their belief and at the same time I resent it. Surveys have shown that they have a much better chance of being happy than those whose belief systems are totally secular- and you can understand why. Everyone's life contains some sadness suffering and disappointments, and they are much easier to accept if you believe there is another life to come in which the imperfections and injustices will be made good; it also makes the business of dying itself a much less depressing prospect. That is why I envy religious believers. There are of course no firm foundations for their beliefs, but you are not allowed to point this out without seeming rude, aggressive and disrespectful- without in fact seeming to attack their right to be happy."

David Lodge's character is talking as a former religious man who used to believe in the afterlife. He understands the real appeal of religion and hope.

I suspect that surveys made in countries where the god-idea and therefore the afterlife is inexistent, where death is part of life, the people are just as happy. In the same way optimism helps; apparently optimists live longer, by many years, than pessimists.

c. The lack of a creator.

Hardly worth mentioning at a time when the scientific discoveries of the universe and the Big Bang theory are pushing the frontier of the known world ever further. The predominance of the monotheistic culture is so invasive that the lack of God feels like a tragedy but only for those who want to believe that. Atheism is just another belief, neither more evil or more virtuous than another, it simply suits different minds. Atheists believe:

"I am a deeply religious non-believer. This is somewhat a new kind of religion." Einstein.

Alternatives.

Christianity, now two thousand years old, has had the field to itself for too long. The voices of the religious has been truly heard, it has been at the detriment of other alternatives. The drive to impose Christianity on a great part of the world since the Cathars has been extremely successful.

The word Catholic has the idea of "universality" in it. More than most this Christian branch has proselytised relentlessly although this particular faith is not more fitting than any other.

To know about alternatives and realise that there are other choices brings tolerance. In the end religion is an individual choice although the pressure of family and friends -the ideology of peers has to be taken into account- and the predominance in the culture and history of the god-idea makes it difficult to discharge.

To accept one's religion from birth is to keep all of one's eggs in an elusive basket. The god-idea in monotheistic religions is not rational; it opens door to unreasonable beliefs. To believe in angels and accept the concepts of saints and miracles is stretching the believable to its extreme but at least these are supposed to be forces for the better. The demons of today are evil; they are devils who punish the defenceless but like witches they are unsubstantial

Similarly the witches of the past had a hard time because many believed in their existence. Today the desire to hang a woman because she is a witch would bring the accuser to a psychiatric hospital because of insanity.

Demons and angels are at the limit of reality but are both extensions of the belief in the god-idea. They belong to the world of fantasy that invades the imagination like fairies, ghosts, vampires and werewolves among others. They can be dangerous. The list of phantoms which are part of the phantasmagoria of the mind is long, imagination has no limit.

One alternative to religions: atheism (or humanism) has the advantage of getting rid of imagination since it is based on reasoning and is not a flight of fancy. Atheism or humanism is one alternative; there are others.

Atheism is: "the theory or belief that God does not exist" and humanism is: "the outlook or system of thought attaching prime importance to human rather than divine or supernatural matters".

A God or no god, religions or atheism are based on unproven beliefs. Therefore both are equally valid sets of beliefs. All beliefs, including atheism, are speculations since there is no proof either way. The growth of each should not be impeded by the others

To consider, to compare and then choose the rational is the reasonable thing to do.The evidences against the god-idea are piling up and numerous evidences against the divine are enough to convince. To use one's reason rather than instinct, imagination or intuition for the vision that guides one's life seems more rational.

What is difficult to remember is that life is full of challenges, rats are everywhere all the time; death is on the other side of the coin, life is death but fortunately there is also there.

Chapter 12.

Communicating.

The Cathars secret, a mystery for so long, had to be solved to be communicated. The Cathars are not vindicated …yet.

Mystery of the Cathars, mystery of the monotheistic religions, mystery of God, mystery of the Holy Spirit, mystery of God made flesh, mystery of the Trinity, mystery of the Resurrection, mystery of the Ascension, mystery of the Assumption, any mysteries irritate and disturb. They seem to say: "you will never know", a challenge that cannot be resisted.

Mysteries fascinate; they pull you with their dangerous tentacles and their attractive unknown. The good ones never divulge their reason to be but like secrets some do not exist, there are figments of the imagination; they are creation of the mind, they are complete fantasy. To know is essential; if curiosity can hurt then information will bring satisfaction.

The Cathars' secret is concrete and discoverable and the whole world can know it.

The Cathars are still with us because they have left so much of them in their region of the Languedoc; they have existed in reality, they are not figments of the imagination; now elusive phantoms they have come back and disturb the living to repair a wrong; their story is unfinished and needs to be redressed. In the quiet streets of Beziers or Carcassonne you can hear their whispers; they are still walking around trying to make themselves heard.

Villegly.

I heard about the Cathars for the first time not far from Carcassonne, a long time ago in the village of Villegly where the medieval castle dominates the small community. Constructed in the 14th century and still in good shape it has acquired Renaissance windows and bigger doors, it is now a grand Town-hall and tourist office. Staying opposite the grey chateau, a fortress of another time, the wish to visit becomes a necessity. The rooms full of paintings, furniture and tapestries tell stories of lost centuries. The desultorily chatter of the few visitors allows questions among the useless ornaments. Our accent from outside the region triggers the exclamation:

"So it's you the French of the north who massacred us nearly a thousand years ago?"

He is talking about the Cathars as if it happened yesterday but in the peace of the day the statement is as shocking as he intended. He does not want an answer and disappears quickly but he has established that if the Cathars are long gone they are not forgotten and neither are the executioners.

The words are extreme, more for effect and shock than an introduction to an interesting conversation but the young man had a grudge and he remembers.

The Cathars are still shouting about an injury done to them, an insult to their good name.

The awareness of their past existence stayed in my mind and rumbled.

The Languedoc

Looking at maps of the Old Languedoc in the 9th century the most striking factor compared to the Languedoc/Roussillon of today is the immense size of the territory. It covered half of what is today's France. It was then a vast, prosperous region with its own culture and its red-bricked capital Toulouse which competed with Rome and Florence. Its independence and wealth completely disappeared in the 14th century.

Its language Occitan, to distinguish it from Languedoc the region, is still spoken in this part of France: Oc for Occitan and for Languedoc, Oc to say yes rather than Oy as it was used in the north of France and which has become "oui" in contempory French.

The Cathars story is now known but the real heart of the Cathars-self, their secret of "no-hell" is still eluding the wide world.

The Cathars are haunting their old land again. In this shimmering land of the Languedoc the Cathar symbol of the cross of the Languedoc crowds the town and villages and assails. The yellow cross floating on red pennants is inescapable and heartbreaking when you know the story behind it. Painted on the walls of streets and drawn on side of shops it materializes in disconcerting places: on tee-shirts and hand-bags, on jars of olives and bottles of wine. I am sure these signs were not here ten years ago or at least I do not remember them. Now it is difficult to avoid them.

Le Chambon sur Lignon.

Le Chambon was a village in the Old Languedoc; it is now in the Vivarais and the department of Haute Loire. A religiously divided village, a village where Camus stayed, a village which lived an extraordinary destiny during the Second World War is now a quiet forgotten place.

The land of the Cathars and the Plateau in the mountain are two places with two peoples with a tenuous link between them. Le Chambon used to be in the Old Languedoc and Villegly is in the Languedoc/Roussillon of today. Both villages have been the centre of dissention about a Christian sect: Villegly was a Cathar village and Le Chambon a Huguenot one. Both places were at the centre of a new faith separating itself from the official Roman Church and both religions have many ideological and theological similarities.

Huguenot is the name given to the Protestants in the 16th century. There is a multitude of explanations for the word Huguenot but the most likely one is a derivation of the German words: "Hugues Genossen" or companions of Hughes. Hugues was a French

Protestant leader in the riots against the Catholic authority in the bilingual Geneva of 1550.

The Protestants like the Cathars opposed the authority of the pope and like them wanted to access the word of God directly. The sacred texts were translated into the vernacular by the Cathars some two hundred years before Luther translated, in German, the New Testament in 1522 and published the complete translation of the bible in 1534. Wycliffe wrote the bible in English in manuscript in 1582 and Tyndale in print in 1586.

The Cathars like the Huguenots and later the Chambonnais had a tendency to rebellion, this intellectual revolt which pushed them not to accept the current thoughts of the day. The Cathars did not accept the rule of the religious minds of the time, the Huguenots did not accept the prescribe worshiping of their God and the Chambonnais did not accept the Nazis' treatment of the Jews. The Chambonnais with the inhabitants of the hamlets around saved 8.000 to 10.000 Jewish children between 1940 and 45. The whole community was involved.

Le Chambon is an isolated place in the Plateau in the mountains of the Cevennes; a strong place for the

Huguenots and at the heart of the religious conflicts during the religious wars which continued till the beginning of the 18th century. It sheltered many dissidents.

The Plateau offered shelter then as it did in 1945; its history explains, in part, the decision of the villagers to risk their lives to save others. The inhabitants remembered that some of them had died or were taken prisoners to preserve their religion. They had lived at first hand the brutality of religious violence. They remembered and had kept a healthy revulsion for religious intolerance.

Le Chambon is an old town, today an ordinary sleepy community with steep streets and a large square; only its history during the Religious wars and the Second World War makes it a place apart.

The two churches, one Catholic and one Protestant: le Temple, sit at odds at the end of a "y" junction close to the river. Between Le Puy and Valence the village nestles in a hollow surrounded by sombre pines.

The records vary but by the end of the war between 8000 and 10,000 children have been rescued. The children arrived at the station where the old steam train had been resurrected and by 1942, after the closure of the internment camps in the rest of France, their numbers increased in an alarming way but the children were always welcomed protected, housed, fed and sent to school.

Andre Trocme was the Reformed Church Minister appointed in the early thirties. His mother was German, his father French, his wife Italian and her father Russian. Edouard Theiss his assistant and best friend was American.

Trocme and Theiss were conscientious objectors and both determined pacifists. They encouraged the parishioners to be aware of the situation against the Jews and of the responsibility of Christians to resist injustices.It was a difficult time; the village was under surveillance but the children were kept safe.

In February 1943 the news of the arrest of the Pasteur Andre Trocme went around the village in minutes.

With him Edouard Theiss and Monsieur Darcissac the director of the primary school were also wanted. The Presbytere, where the family Trocme lived during the war, is near the river on the bend of a narrow street. People gathered in the small space stamping their feet in the snow waiting for their Pasteur. It was cold, several degrees below zero and getting colder in the dusk.

They waited. When Andre Trocme, escorted by the policemen left the house to make his way to the square, the silent crowd followed. Softly at first the villagers started to sing a hymn to say good-by to their minister and friends. On the square milling around the waiting cars, in the cold night the snow flakes falling lazily in the eerie lights amid the sound of voices full of tenderness and worry suspended time.

A lament feeling like an adieu.

The villagers continued to protect the children. Some of the additional helpers in the village became expert at forging false papers. The children sometimes stayed for days, or months or years until a safe passage had been organised for them towards Switzerland.

Finally the war ended and the three men who had been arrested made their way back to Le Chambon. Le Chambon was also the Centre of the Resistance in the region.

"No man is an Island entire of itself;

Everyman is a piece of the Continent, a part of the main;

If a Clod be washed away by sea, Europe is the less;

303

As well as if a Promontory were,

Any man's death diminishes me because I am involved in Mankind".

Poem by John Donne.

Some years later the village was given the tile of Justes by the Jewish organisation of Yad Vashem; usually a certificate to remember individuals for their courageous actions to save Jews. The plaque:

HOMMAGE

A la communauté Protestants de cette terre Cévenole, et a tous ceux entraines par son exemple, croyants de toutes confessions et non-croyants qui pendant la guerre 1939-1945 faisant bloc contre les crimes nazis ont, au péril de leur vie, sous l'occupation caché, protégé, sauvé par milliers tous les persécutés. Les Juifs réfugiés au Chambon sur Lignon et dans les communes avoisinantes.

HOMAGE to the Protestant Community in the land of the Cevennes and to all those following their example believers of all denominations and non-believers toiled together against the Nazis crimes have, at the risk of their life, under the Occupation hidden, protected, saved in thousands all those persecuted. The Jews taking refuge in le Chambon sur Lignon and in the neighbouring villages.

Le Chambon is a place in which the war was survived with dignity and courage. Le Chambon is not alone; endless stories of sacrifices and devotion have been recorded throughout Europe during this last war and thousand of people throughout the world, people of different faiths but of good hearts, have accomplished and are accomplishing daily acts of valour and compassion because they are human.

It was without doubt the love of God which inspired the Chambonnais; they performed the ultimate actualisation of: *love thy neighbour*'s gesture.

But it does not need to belong to monotheism to do good deeds or to experience love for the rest of the world.

Hell is a nuisance, a nasty idea and a powerful concept. Fortunately it can disappear and so render happy those who had been filled with abject terror with the thought of it. Thinking that hell is a joke is better.

When I was young old people had faith; the women in particular seemed to await death with serenity. They had made their peace with God and they knew that a place of light and harmony was going to be their reward when they died.

They believed with all their heart. They had no doubts, the afterlife was a certainty. They believed it. They were happy.

It was difficult not to feel a certain amount of pity and admiration for them; pity because they believed in an illusion, in something that had little probability of being certain but admiration because they were so serene after long and difficult lives; they were contented; to have a soul was reassuring, to have hope was enough.

Monotheism is archaic, it has survived because ideas outside monotheism have been assiduously and cruelly opposed especially by Christianity. The concepts outside monotheism are interpreted as direct attacks against God and therefore are seen as being anti-Christian; until not very long ago to be atheist was to be the enemy.

It is not surprising since atheism denies the existence of God. The predominance of the monotheistic culture has been unreservedly invasive so that the idea that god might not be around feels unnatural. The negative perception and lack of information have hindered the no god-idea to spread effectually.

Believing in one God may be the only way for the religiously minded who cannot conceive of a universe without God. This vision of the world demands compromises and efforts to keep it afloat.

Thousands of years ago our ancestors needed powerful gods to explain their mysterious environment. Gods were terrifying as well as givers of life. But religions and gods die and change, who believes in Zeus or Jupiter and the gaggle of lesser gods on their Mount Olympus?

Is a delusional belief worth preserving for the younger generation? The afterlife is intangible, mysterious, baffling and probably inexistent; it has a 50/50 per cent chance of being a reality if hell is part of the concept but without hell it cannot be. A concept which turns into a fantasy is not worth keeping; the afterlife needs to be remembered only as a historical aberration.

And the best about hell is to discard it forever. The belief in God is convenient, it is too opportune, it suits the human mind too easily to be counted as serious; it is too laced with self-interest. It is time for change.

A large container-ship takes time and space to change direction but the forgetting of hell cannot come too soon.

The Need to Communicate.

There are disadvantages as well as rewards to the monotheistic system. The same applies to the no-god idea. The need to communicate is enhanced by many reasons:

1. The joyful proclamation of the end of hell.

2. Happiness in atheism

3. Morality is not restricted to Christianity in spite of the conviction of monotheists.

4. Religions are not always forces for good.

5. Monotheism is a system with major problems.

1. The Joyful Proclamation of the End of Hell.

Not to believe in hell must bring immense relief to those who were brought up with this terrible notion.

For non- believers the disappearance of the afterlife is not cause for concern since it is a promise, a hope at best and not a certainty. The afterlife is an overrated commodity; a huge question-mark hovers above it. The afterlife is a fiction because it rests on nothing except faith. An afterlife which does not exist is not desired. To miss something that cannot be is not sorrowful. The world of the imagination with its fantasies and dreams is enough.

No afterlife is the joy of no hell.

2. Happiness in Atheism.

Atheists are happy. There is joy of the no-god idea. Life on earth is precious whatever one believes; if that is all there is then every minute counts. To be alive is a marvel; to be aware of being alive is the icing on the cake. The alternative is not to be, not to know, not to feel anything... ever. To think of this void is despair, life is so precious!

To live without gods is exhilarating. To be in control, to be grown up at last, mature, to know that one can survive without divine help is exciting, not to suffer lies, not to be under an illusion, not to be cheated by fantasies result in elation.

Religions help to live better... may be but atheists too have as much happiness as it is possible for each individual to have according to personality and the circumstances of life.

Life on earth is important, valuable, prized, cherished and treasured; it is painful, frustrating, stressful, exhausting, tiresome, demanding and exasperating but always renewed and always changing.

To be an adult brings responsibility but also pleasure, to be an atheist is not for the faint hearted, it needs independence and strength.

To be an atheist is to be alone with one's fellow humans and know that nobody is perfect. To finally release oneself from the constraint of the god-idea is similar to a right of passage. Like youngsters who look forward to becoming independent and responsible adults at last, the atheists are happy because they know themselves to be in control.

Freedom at last! Like the chrysalis into a butterfly stretching its wings and taking flight in the sun the atheist feels ecstasy.... For atheists the realisation that one has reached adulthood and can survive without the guidance of a father is elating. This gained maturity gives pleasure and satisfaction.

Mature, responsible, in charge of himself/herself, and like Sisyphus embracing one specific and personal destiny with full awareness, give happiness. Awareness, maturity, independence and responsibility are the happiness of atheists.

3. Morality is not confined to monotheism.

Atheism lies outside the influence of God's will but it is quite capable of producing individuals and building organisations with excellent secular morality.

The legislation in most religious countries is not controlled by religions but is secular and a matter of State. Laws are guardians of morality and the arbiter of ethics; they do not need religions or God.

Some counties are still controlled by religion. Some areas are influenced by the Islamic faith where Sharia's laws or religious laws are to be the law of the land. Sharia's laws deal with the topics of crimes, policies and economics which are interpreted by Islamic judges with the help of the Koran and sacred texts. The Koran is the Holy book of Islam written 40 or 50 years after the death of the prophet Mohamed and is the authority on ethics. The judges are men only and with this decision of never having women with them half of their world's intelligence is taken out of the equation. These men do not show excessive indulgence in their moral decisions since their guide and Supreme Being Allah is their ultimate model. Allah, like the Christian God is seen as harsh but just with his punishment of hell. The punishments on earth must reflect this intent. In deciding solutions for women that they know less about than the women themselves the Judges must have problems in being understanding and impartial. The women, never having a say in any decisions that concern them have to suffer in silence; they are never appointed to high offices or situations of importance.

In the end the rule of the Imam is obeyed because it is convenient; it gives him power as it does to all who can control the laws.

4. Religions bring conflicts.

Atheism too is at fault; in all fairness atheism itself falls in this category since the Communist communities had no hesitation in going to war.

5. Monotheism is a system with major problems.

Monotheism is a solid system with an awkward structure where all the concepts have to stay together in order for the system to work. The stories of the afterlife, with heaven and hell, are tall stories, even deceptions, certainly not certainties. When investigated monotheism stretches rationality.

It is academically degrading to believe in a system which attacks the rational and demands an elastic imagination. To believe in God is the acceptance of a concept without proof which might bring happiness but which has terrified millions of people for thousand of years because of its spiteful hell.

We are used to the god-idea in the western culture, it is everywhere: in the streets with churches and cathedrals, in schools, in art, in music, in stories, in ceremonies and rituals and even in the old laws; it is in the habit of thinking from the day we are born to the day we die.

It is part of every day and although it is the history and heritage of the past it does not have to be adhered to without consideration.

No regrets are possible with the dismissing of the god-idea when all that is gained is considered. The end of hell is a cause for rejoicing.

Without God love remains; without the god-idea love stays solid.

And love does not need to be adored; it simply needs to be enjoyed, received and given. It is everywhere. To replace a belief in God by a belief in love is to sift one's heart from a fantasy to what is the reality of earth; it is to transfer one's own love from a scheme in the sky to the love of the human world. Yahweh, God and Allah are archaic concepts which have had their uses in a distant but very different past. Synagogues, Churches and Mosques have hollow foundations; their pillars are full of sand. It is time to let them tumble down.

Today Yahweh, God and Allah are obsolete. Religions, whatever forms they take, are not for everybody. Fortunately the picture is changing and humanism is taking its rightful place in our society. Ceremonies, like marriages and funerals, are performed outside religious venues and Good Works are seen to be executed by non- religious organisations. Religions are ways to explain the world; science is another method to experience the universe; philosophies and faiths, with their different approach, are valid too. But is there a need to believe in a mystical force outside the known world?

Passion fills lives. There are numerous passions to choose from; love is high on the list; life is valuable and is a sufficient passion. The list is long: humanity for humanists, the wonderful human brain for biologists and medical enthusiasts; the universe for scientists; there are as many passions as there are individuals.

To be aware that tomorrow will come, that the sun will rise and the day start, that life, in all its variety, will remain, that this idea of continuance, this principle of continuation is with us, is belief enough.

Chapter 13.

Register. Resister.

The idea of doubting old concepts that have been knocking around for ever is useful. Is there a need to believe in anything outside ourselves, like gods, to have a life fulfilled? To assume the necessity of religious beliefs is to lock the box before the lid has been opened. To find what is in the box becomes tricky and opportunities get lost.

Religions are taken for granted; they have been around for as long as history can be remembered. Religions or philosophies of life have dug themselves deeply in the culture they touch. Monotheism is as necessary as air for nearly four billion people but it could be argued that it is more a habit, never contested, than a reality.

How many of these billion have actually made a personal choice about their beliefs? Christianity makes people happy with promises and hope; a belief in an afterlife is a comfort blanket which can alleviate the grief of difficult circumstances. Some mentalities require the consolation of a father-figure but not everybody can take the jump of faith religions demand.

One of the attractions of religions is the reward of routines. Routines make life easier; to follow ones' peers is tempting, to go with the flow is simpler. When there is no need to find different solutions, why bother? This thinking is fine as long as it does not lead to disappointments; what matters is to know, to consider, to have doubts about the given and then... to choose.

The no god-idea is doing well in many countries; in fact it is growing and establishing itself against established religions. Humanist ceremonies: marriages and funerals are officially taking place in dedicated venues with trained orators. They are the symbols that beliefs outside the monotheistic religions are just as valid.

To have doubts about acquired beliefs is important but is only the beginning, resister is the other side of the coin; to resist persuasions is essential too.

"Doubt and "resister" are magic words. The word "Resister" or "register", in old 17th century, is carved on the stone margin of the well in the women's prison in Aigues Mortes. The prisoners were special: young, educated and not criminal, they were imprisoned for their faith. They were Huguenots women mostly from the Cevennes. The men were sent to the galleys.

The Tour de Constance in Aigues Mortes, on the Mediterranean Sea, dominates the sleepy little town. The "Salle des Prisonnieres" where the women stayed till they died can be visited. They carved the word "Register" on the hard stone because they had plenty of time. "Register", Resister, to resist.

They probably used their hair pins, their needles were too valuable to scrape the stone but they persisted and the word is in evidence today. Their only word, their only visible testimony, their cry against authority, aggression, and cruelty.

On a personal note they could have written their cherished title: "Huguenotes" or Protestantes. More generally: they could have chosen the word: "protester" to protest or even more poignantly: Justice. They choose Resister.

The women did not write "Resistez": resist with a Z at the end thus making it an imperative verb, a command, a pressure or an inducement to rebellion. They were careful to choose instead: "resister" with the letter "r" at the end, to resist, a gentler recommendation, a choice. "Resister" is a way of thinking, a state of mind, an appeal for freedom of thoughts. They paid to be different but not one of them changed their mind. They tried to "Resister" because they knew they had no other choice. In their prison they knew that their freedom of conscience was worth giving their life to the idea.

Marie Durand was imprisoned to put pressure on her brother who was a Protestant Minister and although he died a year after her incarceration she was not freed till 38 years alter. Like the other prisoners she had committed no crime except wanting to keep her faith.

The women resisted boredom, depression, illnesses, isolation and enclosure. They resisted against the knowledge of never seeing again their loved ones, of not having children, of not living because they were entombed. I want to follow their example and "resister" like them, resist against prejudices, persecutions and the pestilences of life.

Like the people of "Le Chambon" who in 1940 risked their lives to save the children, I want to belong to the group of silent heroes, unseen and unknown who make a difference.

There are many dedicated and compassionate people in the world who help those in need or fight non-violently for a just cause with or without religions. I try to "Resister" injustices, unkindness, rejection, violence, persuasion to greedy and thoughtless actions and depression.

"Resister" the untruths, myths, propagandas, lies, exaggerations,

"Resister" and like the women in La Tour de Constance to think for myself and take my own decisions. I want be in charge of the life I have chosen like a mature adult. Not always easy but the trying of it is what brings joy.

I want to remember these women with the countless quiet champions of our wonderful world and remember that in a world of more than seven billion there is no need to be alone. I want to remember that among the tragedy of humanity hunger is a persecution too. Pestilences, personal or others need to be contested and combated like Camus suggests. There will always be rats. To live fully with passion or intent, to fight against pestilences in this only life we have, to do the job the best we can is Camus' message.

The alternative to life is no life at all. It is not to live, not to breathe, not to see, to taste, to hear, to touch, to love, not to be, to feel, not to know, not to cry, not to be warm or cold, not be hurt and not to love, not to be loved, not to understand and not to discover more. Imagine the choice: life or nothing!

So life is precious, I cherish it and try to make the most of it; every moment counts because it will end one day always too soon.

I want to make the best of it while it lasts and know that pestilences are suffering and never far away. At least those of us on earth are the lucky ones with the extraordinary chance to be alive. There is no need for more. Life is enough even if it is short.

To believe in life as a principle of continuance, to know that our children and our children's children will be there for a bit longer, is enough. Love, the only thing to increase when it is given.

"I know of only one duty, and that is to love".

A. Camus.